JUST
5
INGREDIENTS

CAKES & DESSERTS

An Hachette UK Company
www.hachette.co.uk

First published in Great Britain in 2015 by
Hamlyn, a division of Octopus Publishing Group Ltd
Endeavour House
189 Shaftesbury Avenue
London WC2H 8JY

Distributed in the US by Hachette Book Group
1290 Avenue of the Americas, 4th and 5th Floors
New York, NY 10020

Distributed in Canada by Canadian Manda Group
664 Annette St., Toronto, Ontario, Canada M6S 2C8

Some of the recipes in this book have previously appeared in other books published
by Hamlyn.

ISBN 978 0 60062 839 2

A CIP catalogue record for this book is available from the British Library

Printed and bound in China

10 9 8 7 6 5 4 3 2 1

Commissioning Editor Eleanor Maxfield
Senior Editor Sybella Stephens
Designers Jeremy Tilston, Jaz Bahra & Eoghan O'Brien
Production Controller Allison Gonsalves

Standard level spoon and cup measurements are used in all recipes.

Eggs should be large unless otherwise stated. The U.S. Food and Drug
Administration advises that eggs should not be consumed raw. This book contains
dishes made with raw or lightly cooked eggs. It is prudent for more vulnerable
people, such as pregnant and nursing mothers, people with a weakened immune
system, the elderly, babies, and young children, to avoid uncooked or lightly
cooked dishes made with eggs. Once prepared, these dishes should be kept
refrigerated and used promptly.

Milk should be whole unless otherwise stated.

Ovens should be preheated to the specific temperature; if using a convection oven,
follow manufacturer's instructions for adjusting the time and the temperature.

All microwave information is based on a 650 watt oven. Follow manufacturer's
instructions for an oven with a different wattage.

This book includes dishes made with nuts and nut derivatives. It is advisable for
customers with known allergic reactions to nuts and nut derivatives and those
who may be potentially vulnerable to these allergies, such as pregnant and nursing
mothers, people with a weakend immune system, the elderly, babies, and children,
to avoid dishes made with nuts and nut oils. It is also prudent to check the labels of
prepared Ingredients for the possible inclusion of nut derivatives.

JUST
5
INGREDIENTS

CAKES & DESSERTS

**MAKE LIFE SIMPLE WITH MORE THAN 100 RECIPES
USING 5 INGREDIENTS OR FEWER**

hamlyn

CONTENTS

INTRODUCTION

The recipes in this book have been chosen not only for their simplicity and great flavors, but also because they use just five or fewer main ingredients.

Applying a five-ingredient approach to cooking will help you create a repertoire of quick, easy adaptable dishes that are not only inexpensive and tasty but that also require little shopping and preparation. You will learn to master some basic recipes in record time and learn to appreciate that cooking for yourself is a satisfying and empowering process.

This approach will make your life easier in three ways. First, because the recipes are straightforward, there is less tedious preparation, which will save you time. Second, you will find that shopping is simpler. How long do you really want to wander around a supermarket searching for something to cook? And third, it will save you money. The five-ingredient approach will mean that you don't have a refrigerator full of half-used packages of odd Ingredients, leftover from previous recipes that you will never use again.

Unlike other five-ingredient cookbooks, you won't have hundreds of hidden added extras to stock up on.

This series requires you to remember only a few pantry

extras—these are simple, easy to remember basics you will no doubt already have on hand.

Start by stocking up on your pantry items (see page 11 and page 13). Make sure you have at least some of them at home all the time so that you know you are just five ingredients away from a decent dessert.

Next, choose a recipe that suits the time you have to cook, your energy levels, and your mood. Check what pantry ingredients you will need on the list. The five key ingredients you will need to buy and complete the dish are clearly numbered.

One of the best ways to eat inexpensively is to avoid costly processed foods. Instead, you should buy basic ingredients, such as vegetables, rice, pasta, fish, and chicken, and build your meals around these. You should also try to avoid waste and not spend money on food you don't eat and that has to be thrown away. Buy food that lasts and plan around the expiration dates of foods. If you have a freezer, freeze the leftovers for another day.

Plan your meals for the week so you need to go shopping only once a week. When you get into the habit of doing this, the ingredients for each meal will be waiting when you need them.

Buy in bulk to get the best prices. Make time to shop around and compare prices in the nearest supermarket, online, your local stores, and on market stalls to see which is cheapest. Try to buy fruit and vegetables when they are in season. Not only will they be better value than exotic produce flown in from abroad but you will be reducing your food miles. Finally, don't even think about spending precious cash on a supermarket's special deal unless it is something you will actually use. Three cans of sardines in mustard sauce for the price of one is a good deal only if you will eat them.

Not many people can resist a cake or a dessert. A good one will brighten you up after a bad day at work, banish the blues, and make a grand finale to a special meal or a welcome alternative gift for a friend.

Of all the different types of cooking, baking cakes continues to thrive as the one we love most. It's a fun, enjoyable way to spend some time and appeals to people of all ages. It's not difficult to see why baking has such enduring popularity—not only does it produce comfort food at its best (who doesn't like a wedge of chocolate cake?), it's also inexpensive and doesn't require advanced culinary knowledge or a kitchen packed with special equipment.

The secret of the perfect dessert is to be sure you have chosen the right one as part of a meal. So if you have a heavy main dish, choose a light, fruity dessert; conversely, a pastry or chocolate dessert can follow a lighter main dish. The time of year will influence your choice, so in winter, you might be craving a warming, comforting dessert whereas in summer something fruitier will probably be your preference. Make use of fruits when they are in season and plentiful; they will taste so much better, even when served simply with a scoop of ice cream or grilled with a sprinkling of sugar.

Short of time? You can cheat and use store-bought puff pastry or rolled dough pie crust. These days, our busy schedules mean

a homemade dessert or cake is a treat instead of an everyday occurrence, but when you do have the time to make one, it is not only immensely rewarding but also a great way to unwind.

WEEKLY PLANNER

SOMETHING TO CELEBRATE

MONDAY
Caramel Ice Cream Cake (see page 98)

TUESDAY
Classic Lemon Tart (see page 102)

WEDNESDAY
Easy Chocolate Fudge Cake (see page 64)

THURSDAY
Strawberry Rosé Gelatin & Syllabub (see page 96)

FRIDAY
Chocolate & Raspberry Soufflés (see page 76)

SATURDAY
Nectarine Brûlée (see page 92)

PANTRY

The only extras you will need!

1 Sugars
2 Flours
3 Oils & vinegars
4 Baking powder
5 Baking soda
6 Salt
7 Lemons & lemon juice

Fruit & nuts
- 1 lemon
- ⅔ cup lemon juice
- 8 oz small strawberries
- 3 nectarines (about 1 lb)
- 2 cups raspberries
- chopped nuts, for decoration

Dairy
- 1 cup mascarpone cheese
- 1½ cups sour cream
- 3 cups heavy cream
- 1 cup light cream
- 1 quart good-quality vanilla ice cream
- 2¼ sticks butter
- nutmeg
- 11 eggs
- 2¼ lb semisweet chocolate
- 8 oz milk chocolate

Jars, cans & packages
- 2¼ cups self-rising flour
- 1¾ cups superfine sugar
- ½ cup packed light brown sugar
- confectiners' sugar
- 8 oz Graham crackers
- 7 oz soft butterscotch fudge
- 1 lb chilled store-bought rolled dough piecrust
- 1 envelope powdered gelatin
- vanilla extract
- rosé wine
- orange liqueur

SUNDAY
Chocolate Millefeuilles (see page 108)

SWEET TREATS ON A BUDGET

MONDAY
Rhubarb Slumps (see page 26)

TUESDAY
Tipsy Berry Waffles (see page 38)

WEDNESDAY
Fig & Honey Cups (see page 54)

THURSDAY
Coconut Syllabub & Almond Brittle (see page 110)

FRIDAY
Blackberry & Apple Puffs (see page 40)

SATURDAY
Golden Raisin & Bran Slice (see page 36)

PANTRY

The only extras you will need!

1 Sugars
2 Flours
3 Oils & vinegars
4 Baking powder
5 Baking soda
6 Salt
7 Lemons & lemon juice

SUNDAY
Chocolate Apple Crepes (see page 84)

SHOPPING LIST:

Fruit, nuts & spices
- 8 rhubarb stalks
- 2 cups mixed berries, such as blueberries, blackberries, and raspberries
- 8 ripe fresh figs
- 2 tablespoons chopped pistachio nuts
- ½ cup slivered almonds
- 1 cup blackberries
- 4 crisp sweet apples
- 1⅓ cups golden raisins
- 15 cardamom seeds, lightly crushed
- 1 tablespoon ground cinnamon
- 1 teaspoon ground allspice

Dairy
- 2 sticks unsalted butter, softened
- 1¾ cups heavy cream
- 2 cups Greek yogurt
- ¼ cup crème fraîche (or extra Greek yogurt)
- 2 cups milk
- 7 eggs

Jars, cans & packages
- 1 cup oats
- ½ cup granulated sugar
- ½ cup Demerara sugar or other raw sugar
- 1 cup superfine sugar
- confectioners' sugar
- 2 tablespoons packed dark brown sugar
- ⅔ cup all-purpose flour
- 1¼ cups self-rising flour
- 2 tablespoons vegetable oil
- 1 cup coconut milk
- ¼ cup honey
- 2 tablespoons molasses
- 2½ cups bran flake cereal
- 2 tablespoons kirsch
- store-bought waffles and pancake mix
- ¼ cup chocolate and hazelnut spread

5 FOR COOLING OFF

What's your favorite way to cool off? Whether you're looking for something refreshing or want to impress guests with a chilled treat, these 5-ingredient recipes prove that frozen desserts can be simple to make.

Tropical Fruit & Basil Ice Cream (see page 28)

Rocky Road Ice Cream Sundaes (see page 122)

Frozen Berry Yogurt Ice Cream (see page 152)

Instant Raspberry Sorbet (see page 58)

Chocolate Ice Cream (see page 68)

5 FOR WARMING UP

For chilly autumnal evenings and cold winter nights, this selection of cakes and desserts will provide comfort for any afternoon or evening, and all using only 5 key ingredients!

Steamed Apple Cake (see page 126)

Rich Chocolate Brownies (see page 150)

Caramel & Date Squares (see page 184)

Sweet Cranberry & Orange Pie (see page 56)

Lemon Puddle Cake (see page 34)

5 FOR MAKING WITH THE KIDS

Cooking and baking is a great opportunity to teach kids all kinds of valuable skills and these recipes with only 5 or less main ingredients are perfect starting points. Have some fun with the kids in the kitchen and get them involved with these easy recipes.

Mile-High Marshmallow Cupcakes (see page 80)

Peanut Butter Cookies (see page 140)

Iced Fig Slice (see page 114)

Baby Butterflies (see page 172)

Chocolate Puddle Cake (see page 82)

5 FOR AFTERNOON SNACKS

Any of these recipes would hit the spot as the perfect midmorning or afternoon snack served with pots of coffee, tea and milk, and with only 5 or less ingredients, they couldn't be simpler.

Chocolate Caramel Shortbread (see page 74)

Chai Tea Bread (see page 104)

Strawberry Lavender Shortbread (see page 116)

Vienesse Whirls (see page 174)

French Macarons (see page 180)

5 FOR A SUMMER PICNIC

These lunch bag or picnic-friendly recipes are perfect for taking alfresco and enjoying in the great outdoors. Just try not to eat them en route!

Fruited Friands (see page 44)

White Chocolate & Apricot Blondies (see page 78)

Spiced Cookies (see page 136)

Mini Custard Tarts (see page 168)

Marsala Raisin Coffee Muffins (see page 178)

5 DINNER PARTY TREATS

Impress your guests with these showstopping desserts, and all using only 5 or less key ingredients!

Chilled Black Current & Mint Soufflés
(see page 42)

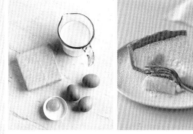

Classic Lemon Tart (see page 102)

Sweet Chestnut Meringue Cups (see page 106)

Coconut Syllabub (see page 110)

Mini Baked Alaskas (see page 138)

FRUITY

Preparation time 20 minutes, plus chilling
Cooking time 25–30 minutes

INGREDIENTS

1 | 1½ sheets frozen puff pastry, thawed

2 | 2 crisp green baking apples (such as Granny Smith), peeled, cored, and sliced

3 | 2 tablespoons unsalted butter, chilled

4 | ice cream, to serve

5 | ¾ cup apricot preserves, to glaze

PANTRY

1 tablespoon superfine sugar; 2 teaspoons lemon juice; 2 teaspoons water

French Apple Flan

■ Divide the pastry into quarters and roll each out on a lightly floured surface until ⅛ inch thick. Using a 5 inch plate as a guide, cut out 4 disks—make a number of short cuts around the plate instead of drawing the knife around it, which can stretch the pastry. Place the pastry disks on a baking sheet.

■ Place a slightly smaller plate on each pastry disk and score around the edge to form a ½ inch border. Prick the centers with a fork and chill for 30 minutes.

■ Arrange the apple slices in a circle over the pastry disks and sprinkle with the sugar. Grate the butter over the top and bake in a preheated oven, at 425°F, for 25–30 minutes, until the pastry and apples are golden.

■ Meanwhile, make an apricot glaze. Put the preserves in a small saucepan with the lemon juice and water and heat gently until the preserves has melted. Increase the heat and boil for 1 minute, remove from the heat, and press through a fine-mesh strainer. Keep warm, then brush over each apple tart while they are still warm. Serve with ice cream.

A PEACHY DELIGHT

For peach tartlets, replace the 2 apples with 2 peaches, halved, skinned, and thinly sliced. Arrange on the pastry circles and continue as opposite, baking for 12–15 minutes.

SERVES 8

Preparation time 20 minutes, plus chilling
Cooking time 33–40 minutes

INGREDIENTS

1	1 chilled store-bought rolled dough piecrust or enough homemade pie dough for a 9 inch pie
2	¾ cup plus 2 tablespoons freshly squeezed lime juice (4–6 limes)
3	8 kaffir lime leaves or the grated zest of 3 limes
4	3 eggs plus 2 egg yolks
5	1½ sticks unsalted butter, softened

PANTRY

a little flour, for dusting; ¾ cup superfine sugar; confectioners' sugar, for dusting

Kaffir Lime Tart

■ Roll out the dough on a lightly floured surface and use it to line a 9 inch tart pan. Prick the bottom with a fork and chill for 30 minutes.

■ Line with nonstick parchment paper, add pie weights or dried beans, and bake in a preheated oven, at 400°F, for 15 minutes. Remove the paper and weights and bake for another 12–15 minutes, until the pastry is crisp and golden. Set aside to cool.

■ Make the filling. Put the sugar, lime juice, and kaffir lime leaves or lime zest in a saucepan and heat gently to dissolve the sugar. Bring to a boil and simmer for 5 minutes. Let cool for 5 minutes, then strain into a clean saucepan.

■ Stir in the eggs, egg yolks, and half the butter and heat gently, stirring, for 1 minute or until the sauce coats the back of the

spoon. Add the remaining butter and whisk constantly until the mixture thickens.

■ Transfer the lime mixture to the pastry crust and bake for 6–8 minutes, until set. Let cool and serve warm dusted with confectioners' sugar.

ADD MORE FRUIT

For mango & kiwifruit salad to serve with the tart, peel, pit, and dice 1 large mango, then mix with 3 peeled and sliced kiwifruits, the seeds scooped from 3 passion fruits, and the juice of 1 lime.

Preparation time 10 minutes
Cooking time 20-25 minutes

INGREDIENTS

1 8 rhubarb stalks, cut into chunks

2 grated zest and juice of 1 orange

3 1½ sticks unsalted butter, softened

4 1 cup rolled oats

5 ⅓ cup heavy cream

PANTRY

⅓ cup superfine sugar; 2 tablespoons packed dark brown sugar

Rhubarb Slumps

■ Mix together the rhubarb, superfine sugar, and orange zest and half the juice in a bowl. Spoon the mixture into 4 individual ramekins.

■ Put the oats, cream, dark brown sugar, and remaining orange juice in the bowl and mix together. Drop spoonfuls of the oat mixture all over the surface of the rhubarb mixture.

■ Set the ramekins on a baking sheet and bake in a preheated oven, at 350°F, for 20-25 minutes, until the topping is browned. Serve hot.

MAKE IT CRISPY

For apple and blackberry crisps, peel, core, and chop 2 sweet, crisp apples, then mix with ⅔ cup blackberries, ⅓ cup superfine sugar, and 1 tablespoon apple juice. Spoon into the ramekins as above. Sift 1 cup all-purpose flour into a bowl, add 4 tablespoons butter, diced, and rub in with the fingertips until the mixture resembles coarse bread crumbs. Stir in ¼ cup dark brown sugar, ⅔ cup bran flakes, and ½ cup chopped mixed nuts. Spoon the mixture over the fruit and flatten slightly with the back of a spoon. Bake as opposite until the topping is lightly golden.

Preparation time 10 minutes
Cooking time none

INGREDIENTS

1 3 cups frozen tropical fruits, such as mango, papaya, and pineapple

2 1 tablespoon lime juice

3 ¾ cup mascarpone cheese

4 2 tablespoons chopped basil, plus 4-6 basil sprigs, to decorate

PANTRY

2 tablespoons confectioners' sugar

Tropical Fruit & Basil Ice Cream

■ Place half the fruit and the lime juice in a food processor and process until coarsely chopped. Add the mascarpone and confectioners' sugar and blend until fairly smooth.

■ Add the remaining fruit and the basil and pulse until no large lumps of fruit remain. Scoop into bowls and serve immediately, decorated with basil sprigs.

Preparation time 15 minutes, plus standing
Cooking time 25 minutes

INGREDIENTS

1   **3 tablespoons unsalted butter**

2   **1 egg, plus 1 egg yolk**

3   **few drops vanilla extract**

4   **⅔ cup mixed milk and water**

5   **1 (15 oz) can apricot halves, drained**

PANTRY

⅓ cup all-purpose flour; 2 tablespoons superfine
sugar; grated zest of ½ lemon; confectioners'
sugar, for dusting

Apricot Clafouti

■ Sift the flour into a bowl and add the
sugar and lemon zest. Melt 2 tablespoons
of the butter, then add to the flour with the
whole egg, egg yolk, and vanilla extract.
Gradually beat in the milk and water until
smooth. Let stand for 30 minutes or longer.

■ Grease liberally 4 individual ¾ cup metal
dessert molds with the remaining butter.
Quarter the apricots and divide among the
molds. Stand the molds on a baking sheet,
then cook in a preheated oven, at 375°F, for
5 minutes.

■ Pour the batter quickly into the dessert
molds so that the mix sizzles in the hot
butter. Bake for about 20 minutes, until
well risen and golden brown. Dust the tops
with sifted confectioners' sugar and serve
immediately, because the desserts will sink
as they cool.

TRY CHERRIES

For cherry clafouti, make the batter with the grated zest of ½ orange instead of the lemon. Divide 2 cups of drained, canned morello cherries in syrup between the dessert molds as opposite. Bake the fruit and then add the batter as opposite.

Preparation time 25 minutes, plus cooling
Cooking time 1 hour 5 minutes

INGREDIENTS

1   **2 (15 oz) cans pitted black or red cherries**

2   **1 teaspoon ground allspice**

3   **1½ sticks salted butter, chilled and diced**

4   **½ cup ground almonds (almond meal)**

5   **1 egg**

PANTRY

2 teaspoons cornstarch; 2 cups all-purpose flour; 2 teaspoons baking powder; ¾ cup plus 2 tablespoons superfine sugar

Cherry Crumb Cake

■ Drain the cherries, reserving 7 tablespoons of the juice. Put a little of the reserved juice into a small saucepan with the cornstarch and blend until smooth. Add the remaining juice and bring to a boil, stirring. Add the cherries and cook, stirring, for about 1 minute or until thickened slightly. Let cool.

■ Put the flour, baking powder, and allspice into a bowl or food processor. Add the butter and rub in with fingertips or process until the mixture resembles bread crumbs. Add the sugar and ground almonds and mix or blend again until the mixture resembles a coarse crumb mix. Reserve 2 cups of the mixture. Add the egg to the remaining mixture and mix to a soft dough.

■ Turn the dough into a greased 8½–9 inch square shallow baking pan and press it into the corners and slightly up the sides.

Spread over the cherries to ¾ inch from the edges, then sprinkle with the reserved crumb mixture.

■ Bake in a preheated oven, at 350°F, for about 1 hour, until the crumb topping is golden. Let cool in the pan, then cut into squares to serve.

USE APRICOTS

For apricot crumb cake, put 1¾ cup coarsely chopped dried apricots, ⅔ cup apple or orange juice, and 1½ teaspoons ground ginger in a saucepan. Bring to a boil, then reduce the heat and cook very gently for 5 minutes. Blend 1½ teaspoons cornstarch with 2 tablespoons water and add to the pan. Cook, stirring, for 2 minutes, until thickened slightly. Let cool. Make the cake opposite, omitting the allspice and using the apricot mixture instead of the cherries.

SERVES 4

Preparation time 20 minutes
Cooking time 25 minutes

INGREDIENTS

1 6 tablespoons unsalted butter, at room temperature

2 3 eggs, separated

3 1¼ cup milk

PANTRY

¾ cup superfine sugar; grated zest of 2 lemons, plus juice from 1 lemon; ⅓ cup plus 1 tablespoon all-purpose flour; ¼ teaspoon baking powder; confectioners' sugar, for dusting (optional)

Lemon Puddle Cake

■ Use some of the butter to lightly grease a 1¼ quart baking dish, then stand the dish in a roasting pan. Put the rest of the butter in a mixing bowl with the superfine sugar and lemon zest. Beat the egg whites in a separate bowl until they form soft peaks. Using the still dirty mixer, beat the butter, sugar, and lemon zest until light and fluffy, then mix in the flour, baking powder, and egg yolks.

■ Mix in the milk and lemon juice gradually until only just mixed. The mixture may appear to separate slightly but this will disappear during baking.

■ Fold in the egg whites, then gently pour the mix into the greased dish. Pour hot water from the faucet into the roasting pan to come halfway up the sides of the dish.

■ Cook in a preheated oven, at 375°F, for about 25 minutes, until slightly risen, golden brown, and the top has begun to crack. Insert a knife into the center—the top two-thirds should be soufflelike and the bottom third a saucy, custardlike layer. If it's soft in the center, cook for an extra 5 minutes.

■ Dust the top with a little sifted confectioners' sugar, if desired, then serve immediately spooned into shallow bowls. Don't let the dessert stand or the topping will absorb the sauce.

MAKE IT ORANGE

For Grand Marnier cake, use the grated zest of 1 large orange instead of the lemon zest and replace the lemon juice with 3 tablespoons Grand Marnier. Cook as opposite.

Preparation time 10 minutes, plus standing
Cooking time 45 minutes

INGREDIENTS

1	1⅓ cups golden raisins
2	2 tablespoons molasses
3	2½ cups shredded bran or bran flake cereal
4	1 teaspoon ground allspice
5	1¼ cups milk

PANTRY

⅔ cup Demerara or other raw sugar, plus extra for sprinkling; 1¼ cups all-purpose flour; 1¼ teaspoons baking powder

Golden Raisin & Bran Slice

■ Mix together the golden raisins, sugar, molasses, bran, allspice, and milk in a bowl. Let stand for 20 minutes to allow the bran to soften. Stir in the flour and baking powder.

■ Transfer the mixture into a greased and lined 9 x 5 x 3 inch or 1¼ quart loaf pan and level the surface. Bake in a preheated oven, at 325°F, for about 45 minutes or until risen, firm to the touch, and a toothpick inserted into the center comes out clean. Loosen the cake at the ends and transfer to a wire rack. Peel off the lining paper and let cool. Cut into slices and spread with a little butter to serve.

ADD FIGS

For gingered fig slice, make the cake as opposite, replacing the golden raisins with 1 cup sliced dried figs, the molasses with 2 tablespoons honey, and the allspice with 1 piece of preserved ginger in syrup, finely chopped. Serve drizzled with extra honey.

SERVES 4

Preparation time 5 minutes
Cooking time 1–2 minutes

INGREDIENTS

1	1 tablespoon butter
2	2 cups mixed berries, such as blueberries, blackberries, and raspberries
3	2 tablespoons kirsch
4	4 waffles
5	¼ cup crème fraîche or whipped cream

PANTRY

1 tablespoon superfine sugar

Tipsy Berry Waffles

■ Melt the butter in a nonstick skillet, add the berries, sugar, and kirsch, and cook over high heat, stirring gently, for 1–2 minutes.

■ Meanwhile, toast or reheat the waffles according to the package directions. Put a waffle on each serving plate, spoon the berries over the waffles, and top each portion with 1 tablespoon crème fraîche or whipped cream. Serve immediately.

Preparation time 15 minutes
Cooking time 20 minutes

INGREDIENTS

1 1 teaspoon ground cinnamon

2 1 cup milk

3 2 extra-large eggs

4 1 cup blackberries

5 1 small sweet, crisp apple, cored and cut into thin slices

PANTRY

2 tablespoons vegetable oil; ⅔ cup all-purpose flour; pinch of salt; ¼ cup superfine sugar, plus 1 tablespoon; confectioners' sugar, for dusting

Blackberry & Apple Puffs

■ Liberally brush a 12-cup muffin pan with the oil. Place in a preheated oven, at 350°F, to heat.

■ Meanwhile, sift the flour, cinnamon, and salt into a large bowl. Stir in the ¼ cup sugar and make a well in the center. Whisk together the milk and eggs in a small bowl, then gradually whisk into the flour to form a smooth batter.

■ Remove the hot muffin pan from the oven and pour in the batter. Add a couple of blackberries in the centers, then top with apple slices and sprinkle with the 1 tablespoon sugar.

■ Return to the oven and cook for 20 minutes or until risen, golden, and cooked through. Serve dusted with confectioners' sugar.

ADD A SAUCE

For a blackberry sauce, place 2 cups blackberries, 2 tablespoons superfine sugar, and the grated zest and juice of 1 lemon in a saucepan and heat gently for 5–6 minutes, until the fruit starts to burst. Serve warm with spoonfuls of vanilla yogurt.

SERVES 6

Preparation time 40 minutes, plus chilling
Cooking time 18–20 minutes

INGREDIENTS

1 1¾ cups black currants or blueberries,
defrosted if frozen

2 4 teaspoons powdered gelatin

3 4 eggs, separated

4 1 cup heavy cream

5 ⅓ cup finely chopped fresh mint

PANTRY

⅓ cup water; 1 cup superfine sugar; confectioners'
sugar, for dusting

Chilled Black Currant & Mint Souffle

■ Wrap a double thickness strip of nonstick parchment paper around a 5½ inch diameter × 2½ inch deep souffle dish so the paper stands 2½ inches above the dish top. Put the black currants or blueberries and 2 tablespoons of the water in a saucepan, cover, and cook gently for 5 minutes, until softened. Blend until smooth, then press through a strainer.

■ Put the remaining water into a small heatproof bowl and sprinkle the gelatin over it, making sure the water absorbs all the powder. Set aside for 5 minutes, then stand the bowl in a saucepan filled halfway with boiling water and simmer for 3–4 minutes, stirring occasionally, until the gelatin dissolves to a clear liquid.

■ Put the egg yolks and superfine sugar into a large heatproof bowl and place over a saucepan of simmering water, making sure the bottom of the bowl is not touching

the water. Whisk for 10 minutes or until the yolks are thick and pale, and they leave a trail when lifted above the mixture. Remove from the heat and continue whisking until cool. Fold in the dissolved gelatin in a thin, steady stream, then fold in the puree.

■ Whip the cream softly, then fold into the souffle mix with the mint. Whisk the whites into stiff, moist-looking peaks. Fold a large spoonful into the souffle mixture to loosen it, then gently fold in the remaining whites. Pour the mixture into the souffle dish so that it stands above the rim of the dish. Chill for 4 hours or until set.

■ Remove the string and paper. To decorate, arrange 4–5 strips of nonstick parchment paper over the souffle top so some overlap, then dust with sifted confectioners' sugar. Lift off the strips and serve immediately or the sugar will dissolve.

MAKES 12

Preparation time 20 minutes, plus cooling
Cooking time 25 minutes

INGREDIENTS

1 1½ sticks unsalted butter

2 ½ cup dried strawberries, sour cherries, or cranberries coarsely chopped

3 2 tablespoons orange juice

4 6 egg whites

5 1¼ cups ground almonds (almond meal)

PANTRY

2 cups plus 2 tablespoons superfine sugar, plus extra for sprinkling; ⅔ cup all-purpose flour

Fruited Friands

■ Melt the butter and let cool. Put the dried strawberries, cherries, or cranberries and orange juice into a saucepan and heat until hot, then transfer to a bowl and let cool.

■ Whisk the egg whites in a large clean bowl with a handheld electric mixer until frothy and increased in volume but not peaking. Add the sugar, flour, and ground almonds and stir in until almost combined. Drizzle the melted butter over the mixture, then stir together gently until just combined.

■ Divide the batter evenly among the cups of a greased 12-cup muffin pan, then sprinkle the strawberries, cherries, or cranberries on top. Bake in a preheated oven, at 400°F, for about 20 minutes, until pale golden and just firm to the touch. Let stand in the pan for 5 minutes, then transfer to a wire rack to cool. Serve sprinkled with superfine sugar.

A NUTTY VERSION

For hazelnut friands, put 1¼ cups blanched hazelnuts in a food processor or blender and process until the consistency of ground almonds. Finely chop another ¼ cup hazelnuts. Make the friands as opposite, adding ½ teaspoon ground cinnamon when melting the butter, omitting the strawberries and orange juice and replacing the ground almonds with the ground hazelnuts. Spoon the mixture into the pan and sprinkle with the chopped hazelnuts. Bake as opposite.

SERVES 8

Preparation time 40 minutes, plus freezing
Cooking time 20–25 minutes

INGREDIENTS

1	6 tablespoons unsalted butter
2	½ teaspoon ground allspice
3	3 small mangoes, peeled, pitted, and thickly sliced
4	1 sheet chilled store-bought puff pastry

PANTRY

⅓ cup grated palm sugar or dark brown sugar; a little flour, for dusting

Mango & Palm Sugar Tatin

■ Make the topping. Heat the butter, sugar, and spice together in a 9 inch ovenproof skillet until the butter has melted. Remove the pan from the heat. Carefully arrange the mango slices in the pan, fanning them from the center outward to make 2 layers.

■ Roll out the pastry on a lightly floured surface and trim to a disk a little larger than the size of the pan. Press it down over the mangoes and into the edges of the pan and pierce a small hole in the center. Bake in a preheated oven, at 425°F, for 20–25 minutes, until the pastry is risen and golden. Let stand for 10 minutes before turning out onto a large plate. Serve with ice cream.

MAKES 4

Preparation time 30 minutes
Cooking time 20–25 minutes

INGREDIENTS

1 3 cups fresh trimmed gooseberries or 1 (16 oz) can gooseberries, drained

2 2 sheets store-bought rolled dough piecrust or enough homemade pie dough for two 7 inch pies

3 1 tablespoon elderflower syrup (cordial)

4 milk or beaten egg, to glaze

PANTRY

⅔ cup superfine sugar, plus extra for sprinkling; 2 teaspoons cornstarch

Gooseberry & Elderflower Pies

■ Mix together the sugar, cornstarch, and gooseberries in a bowl. Cut the dough into 2 pieces, then roll each piece out to about a 7 inch circle. Drape each piece into a buttered individual tart pan, 4 inches in diameter and 1 inch deep, leaving the excess dough overhanging the edges of the pans.

■ Spoon in the gooseberry mixture and mound up in the center, then drizzle over the elderflower syrup. Fold the overhanging dough up and over the filling, pleating where needed and leaving the centers of the pies open.

■ Brush the dough with milk or beaten egg, sprinkle with a little sugar, and bake in a preheated oven, at 375°F, for 20–25 minutes, until golden. Let stand for 15 minutes, then serve with elderflower cream (see opposite).

MAKE AN ELDERFLOWER CREAM

For elderflower cream, to serve
as an accompaniment, whip
1 cup heavy cream, then fold in
2 tablespoons elderflower syrup
(cordial, available online) and the
grated zest of ½ lemon.

SERVES 6

Preparation time 30 minutes
Cooking time 20–25 minutes

INGREDIENTS

1   **1 (1 lb) package chilled store-bought puff pastry**

2   **4 ripe peaches or nectarines, thickly sliced**

3   **1 cup blueberries**

4   **1 egg, beaten**

PANTRY

a little flour, for dusting; ¼ cup superfine sugar, plus extra to decorate; grated zest of ½ lemon; confectioners' sugar, for dusting

Peach & Blueberry Jalousie

■ Roll out half the pastry on a lightly floured surface and trim to a 12 × 7 inch rectangle. Transfer to a lightly greased baking sheet.

■ Pile the peach or nectarine slices on top, leaving a 1 inch border of dough showing, then sprinkle the blueberries, sugar, and lemon zest over the fruit. Brush the dough border with a little beaten egg.

■ Roll out the remaining dough to a little larger than the first piece, then trim to 13 × 8 inches. Fold in half lengthwise, then make cuts in from the fold about ½ inch apart and about 2½ inches long, leaving a wide uncut border of dough.

■ Lift the dough over the fruit, unfold so that the fruit and bottom layer of dough are completely covered, then press the dough edges together. Trim if needed.

■ Press together the pastry edges with a knife. Flute the edges by pressing the first and second finger onto the pie edge, then make small cuts with a knife between them to create a scalloped edge.

■ Brush the top of the dough with beaten egg, sprinkle with a little extra sugar, and bake in a preheated oven, at 400°F, for 20–25 minutes, until the pastry is well risen and golden brown. Serve cut into squares, warm or cold, with cream or ice cream.

A SEASONAL FILLING

For apple & blackberry jalousie, replace the peaches and blueberries with 4 Granny Smith apples, cored, quartered, and thickly sliced, and 1 cup blackberries.

CUTS INTO 8

Preparation time 40 minutes
Cooking time 35–45 minutes

INGREDIENTS

1   4 egg whites

2   ¼ teaspoon cream of tartar

3   ½ cup walnut pieces, lightly toasted and chopped

4   ¾ cup plus 2 tablespoons heavy cream

5   8 oz strawberries

PANTRY

⅔ firmly packed light brown sugar; ½ cup superfine sugar; 1 teaspoon white wine vinegar

Strawberry Meringue Cake

■ Whisk the egg whites and cream of tartar in a large clean bowl until stiff. Combine the sugars, then gradually whisk into the egg white, a little at a time, until it has all been added. Whisk for another few minutes until the meringue mixture is thick and glossy. Fold in the white wine vinegar, then fold in the walnuts.

■ Divide the meringue mixture evenly between 2 greased 8 inch cake pans with the bottoms lined with nonstick parchment paper. Spread the surfaces level, then swirl the tops with the back of a spoon. Bake in a preheated oven, at 300°F, for 35–45 minutes, until lightly browned and crisp. Loosen the edges and let cool in the pans.

■ Reloosen the edges of the meringues and turn out onto 2 clean dish towels. Peel off the lining paper, then put one of the meringues on a serving plate.

■ Whip the cream until forming soft peaks, then spoon three-quarters over the meringue. Halve 8 of the smallest strawberries and set aside. Hull and slice the rest and arrange on the cream. Cover with the second meringue, top uppermost. Decorate with spoonfuls of the remaining cream and the reserved halved strawberries. Serve within 2 hours of assembly.

SERVES 4

Preparation time 10 minutes, plus chilling
Cooking time none

INGREDIENTS

| 1 | 6 ripe fresh figs, thinly sliced |

| 2 | 2 cups Greek yogurt |

| 3 | ¼ cup honey |

| 4 | 2 tablespoons chopped pistachio nuts |

Fig & Honey Desserts

■ Arrange the fig slices snugly in the bottom of 4 glasses or glass bowls. Spoon the yogurt over the figs and chill in the refrigerator for 10–15 minutes.

■ Just before serving, drizzle 1 tablespoon honey over each dessert and sprinkle the pistachio nuts on top.

SERVES 6-8

Preparation time 30 minutes, plus cooling
Cooking time 35–40 minutes

INGREDIENTS

1	5 cups frozen cranberries
2	grated zest and juice of 1½ oranges
3	1 (1 lb) package store-bought puff pastry, defrosted if frozen
4	beaten egg, to glaze

PANTRY

¾ cup superfine sugar; 2 tablespoons water;
1 tablespoon cornstarch; ¾ cup confectioners'
sugar, sifted

Sweet Cranberry & Orange Pie

■ Cook the cranberries in a saucepan with the sugar, zest and juice from 1 orange (reserving the rest for decoration), and the measured water for 10 minutes, stirring occasionally until the cranberries are soft. Mix the cornstarch to a paste with a little extra water, add to the cranberries, and cook for a few minutes, stirring until thickened, then let cool.

■ Cut the pastry in half, roll out one half on a lightly floured surface, and trim to an 8 × 10 inch rectangle, then transfer to a buttered baking sheet. Brush the egg in a border around the edge of the rectangle, then pile the cranberry mixture in the middle.

■ Roll out the remaining pastry a little larger than the first and drape over the cranberries. Press the pastry edges together to seal well, then trim the top pastry layer to match the lower one. Press together the edges of the pastry, then flute.

■ Brush the top with egg, then bake in a preheated oven, at 400°F, for 25–30 minutes, until well risen and golden brown. Let cool for 30 minutes.

■ Mix the confectioners' sugar with enough of the remaining orange juice to make a smooth icing that just falls from a spoon, then drizzle randomly over the pie to decorate and sprinkle with the remaining grated orange zest. Set aside for 20 minutes or until the icing is set, then cut into strips to serve.

TRY MIXED BERRIES

For mixed berry pie, cook a 1 lb bag of mixed frozen berries with ½ cup superfine sugar and the zest and juice of 1 orange, but no extra water. Thicken with cornstarch and finish as above, dusting the top with confectioners' sugar instead of drizzling with the icing.

Preparation time 5 minutes
Cooking time none

INGREDIENTS

 2½ cups frozen raspberries

 1 tablespoon crème de framboise (raspberry liqueur; optional)

 fresh raspberries, to serve

PANTRY

2 tablespoons superfine sugar; 2 tablespoons water

Instant Raspberry Sorbet

■ Put the raspberries, sugar, measured water, and crème de framboise, if using, into a food processor. Process for 2–3 minutes, until all the ingredients are blended and start to come together.

■ Serve scoops of sorbet immediately in bowls with fresh raspberries, or place in a freezerproof container and freeze until ready to use.

SERVE WITH CHOCOLATE CONES

Melt 2 oz semisweet chocolate, broken into small pieces, in a heatproof bowl set over a saucepan of gently simmering water. Remove from the heat and dip the ends of 4 ice cream cones into the melted chocolate, then roll the ends in ⅓ cup chopped pistachios. Stand in glasses and chill until set. Make the raspberry sorbet as opposite and serve scoops in the cones.

Preparation time 20 minutes
Cooking time 35 minutes

INGREDIENTS

1 1 stick unsalted butter, softened

2 2 extra-large eggs, beaten

3 1 cup ground almonds (almond meal)

4 3 ripe pears, peeled, halved, and cored

5 ½ cup slivered almonds

PANTRY

⅔ cup superfine sugar; ⅓ cup all-purpose flour, sifted; ½ teaspoon baking powder; sifted confectioners' sugar, for dusting

Pear & Almond Cake

■ Beat together the butter and superfine sugar in a bowl until pale and fluffy. Add the eggs, a little at a time, beating well after each addition. If the mixture starts to curdle, add 1 tablespoon of the flour. Fold in the flour, ground almonds, and baking powder, using a large metal spoon.

■ Spoon the batter into a greased 8 inch springform cake pan and level the surface. Arrange the pear halves over the top and bake in a preheated oven, at 375°F, for 25 minutes. Sprinkle the slivered almonds over the top and return to the oven for another 10 minutes, until a toothpick inserted into the center comes out clean.

■ Let cool in the tin, then carefully remove the ring and bottom and dust with confectioners' sugar. Serve with Mascarpone, Marsala & Orange Cream, if desired (see opposite).

ADD A SWEET CREAM

For mascarpone, Marsala & orange cream, to serve as an accompaniment, whisk together the grated zest of 1 orange and 2 tablespoons orange juice, 2 tablespoons sweet Marsala, and ½ cup mascarpone cheese in a bowl. Sweeten with sifted confectioners' sugar to taste.

CHOCOLATE

INGREDIENTS

1	14 oz semisweet chocolate, broken into pieces

2	1¾ sticks butter

3	4 eggs, beaten

4	⅔ cup light cream

PANTRY

⅔ cup superfine sugar; 1¾ cups all-purpose flour,
sifted; 1¾ teaspoons baking powder

Easy Chocolate Fudge Cake

■ Grease an 8 × 12 inch baking pan lightly and line the bottom and sides with nonstick parchment paper. Put 8 oz of the chocolate with the butter into a heatproof bowl set over a saucepan of gently simmering water (don't let the bowl touch the water) and stir over low heat until melted. Let cool for 5 minutes.

■ Whisk together the eggs and sugar in a bowl for 5 minutes, until thick, while the cake is cooking. Beat in the cooled chocolate mixture and fold in the flour and baking powder.

■ Spoon the batter into the prepared pan and bake in a preheated oven, at 325°F, for 45–50 minutes, until risen and firm to the touch. Let cool in the pan for 10 minutes, then turn out onto a wire rack to cool completely, removing the paper from the cake.

■ Meanwhile, make the icing. Put the remaining 6 oz chocolate into a saucepan with the cream and heat gently, stirring, until melted. Let cool for 1 hour until thickened to a pouring consistency, then spread over the cake. Let set for 30 minutes before serving.

MAKES 16

Preparation time 10 minutes
Cooking time 15 minutes

INGREDIENTS

1   **1 stick unsalted butter, softened**

2   **1 teaspoon vanilla extract**

3   **1 egg, lightly beaten**

4   **1 tablespoon milk**

5   **1½ cups semisweet chocolate chips**

PANTRY

¾ cup firmly packed light brown sugar; 1⅔ cups
all-purpose flour; 1 teaspoon baking powder

Chocolate Chip Cookies

■ Beat together the butter and sugar
in a large bowl until pale and fluffy. Mix in
the vanilla, then gradually beat in the egg,
beating well after each addition. Stir in the
milk. Sift in the flour and baking powder,
then fold in. Stir in the chocolate chips.

■ Drop level tablespoonfuls of the dough,
about 1½ inches apart, onto a large baking
sheet lined with parchment paper, then
lightly press with a floured fork. Bake in a
preheated oven, at 350°F, for 15 minutes
or until lightly golden brown. Transfer to
a wire rack to cool.

SERVES 4

Preparation time 20 minutes,
plus cooling and freezing
Cooking time 10 minutes

INGREDIENTS

1	1¼ cups heavy cream

2	2 tablespoons milk

3	½ teaspoon vanilla extract

4	9 oz bittersweet chocolate, broken into pieces

5	2 tablespoons light cream

PANTRY

⅓ cup confectioners' sugar, sifted; ⅔ cup water;
3 tablespoons superfine sugar

Chocolate Ice Cream

■ Put the heavy cream and milk into a bowl and whisk until just stiff. Stir in the confectioners' sugar and vanilla extract. Pour the mixture into a shallow freezer container and freeze for 30 minutes or until the ice cream begins to set around the edges. (This ice cream cannot be made in an ice cream machine.)

■ Melt 4 oz of the chocolate with the light cream in a heatproof bowl set over a saucepan of barely simmering water, making sure the bottom of the bowl does not touch the water. Stir until smooth, then set aside to cool.

■ Remove the ice cream from the freezer and spoon into a bowl. Add the melted chocolate and quickly stir it through the ice cream with a fork. Return the ice cream to the freezer container, cover, and freeze until set. Transfer the ice cream to the refrigerator 30 minutes before serving, to soften slightly.

■ Heat the water, superfine sugar, and remaining chocolate together gently in a saucepan, stirring until melted. Serve immediately with scoops of the ice cream.

MAKES 12

Preparation time 20 minutes
Cooking time 20 minutes

INGREDIENTS

1 | 3 tablespoons mint leaves

2 | 1 stick salted butter, softened

3 | 2 eggs

4 | 6 oz white chocolate, chopped

PANTRY

½ cup superfine sugar; 1¼ cups all-purpose flour; 1¾ teaspoons baking powder; confectioners' sugar, for dusting

Minted White Chocolate Cakes

■ Line a 12-cup muffin pan with paper cupcake liners.

■ Put the mint leaves into a heatproof bowl, cover with boiling water, and let stand for 30 seconds. Drain and pat dry on paper towels. Put the leaves in a food processor with the superfine sugar and process until the mint is finely chopped.

■ Transfer the mint sugar to a bowl and add the butter, eggs, flour, and baking powder. Beat with a handheld electric mixer for about a minute until light and creamy.

■ Stir in 3½ oz of the chocolate and then divide the cake batter among the paperliners. Sprinkle with the remaining chocolate.

■ Bake in a preheated oven, at 350°F, for 20 minutes or until the cakes are risen and just firm to the touch. Transfer to a wire rack to cool. Lightly dust with confectioners' sugar.

CUTS INTO 8

Preparation time 20 minutes
Cooking time 50 minutes

INGREDIENTS

1 1 stick salted butter, softened

2 2 eggs

3 ⅓ cup unsweetened cocoa powder

4 15 oz milk chocolate, chopped into ¼ inch pieces, plus 2 oz, broken into pieces

5 4 tablespoons unsalted butter, softened

PANTRY

⅔ cup firmly packed light brown sugar; 1 cup all-purpose flour; 1 teaspoon baking powder ⅔ cup confectioners' sugar, sifted

Chocolate Chip Tea Bread

■ Grease an 8½ x 4½ x 2½ inch or 3 cup loaf pan and line the bottom and sides with nonstick parchment paper.

■ Beat together the salted butter, sugar, eggs, flour, baking powder, and cocoa powder in a bowl until smooth and creamy. Add 4 oz of the chopped chocolate to the bowl. Mix well.

■ Spoon the batter into the prepared pan and level the surface. Bake in a preheated oven, at 325°F, for about 50 minutes or until firm to the touch and a toothpick inserted into the center comes out clean. Loosen the cake at the ends and transfer to a wire rack. Peel off the lining paper and let cool.

■ Make the buttercream. Melt the broken pieces of chocolate in a heatproof bowl set over a saucepan of gently simmering water, making sure the bottom of the bowl does not touch the water. Meanwhile, beat together the unsalted butter and confectioners' sugar in a bowl until pale and creamy. Beat in the melted chocolate. Spread the buttercream over the top of the cake and sprinkle with the reserved chopped chocolate.

CUTS INTO 15

Preparation time 20 minutes, plus chilling
Cooking time 15 minutes

INGREDIENTS

1 **7 tablespoons butter, at room temperature, plus 7 tablespoons butter**

2 **1 (14 oz) can condensed milk**

3 **3½ oz white chocolate, broken into pieces**

4 **3½ oz semisweet chocolate, broken into pieces**

PANTRY

¼ cup superfine sugar; ⅔ cup brown rice flour;
¾ cup cornstarch; ¼ cup firmly packed light
brown sugar

Chocolate Caramel Shortbread

■ Beat the butter at room temperature and the superfine sugar together in a mixing bowl until pale and creamy, then stir in the brown rice flour and cornstarch until well combined. Press the shortbread into an 11 × 7 inch baking pan, then bake in a preheated oven, at 400°F, for 10–12 minutes, until golden.

■ Meanwhile, place the remaining butter, light brown sugar, and condensed milk in a heavy saucepan and heat over low heat until the sugar has dissolved, then cook for 5 minutes, stirring continuously until just beginning to darken. Remove from the heat and let cool a little, then pour the caramel over the shortbread base and let cool completely.

■ For the topping, melt the white and semisweet chocolate in separate heatproof bowls set over saucepans of simmering water, making sure the bottom of the bowls do not touch the water. When the caramel is firm, spoon alternate spoonfuls of the white and dark chocolate over the caramel, tap the pan on the work surface so that the different chocolates merge, then use a knife to make swirls in the chocolate. Refrigerate until set, then cut into 15 pieces.

INGREDIENTS

 1   3½ oz semisweet chocolate

2   3 eggs, separated

3   1¼ cups raspberries, plus extra to serve (optional)

PANTRY

⅓ cup all-purpose flour, sifted; ¼ teaspoon baking powder; 3½ tablespoons superfine sugar; confectioners' sugar sifted, to decorate

Chocolate & Raspberry Souffles

■ Break the chocolate into squares and put them in a large heatproof bowl over a saucepan of simmering water. Let heat until melted, then remove from the heat and let cool a little. Whisk in the egg yolks and fold in the flour and baking powder.

■ Whisk the egg whites and superfine sugar in a medium bowl until they form soft peaks. Beat a spoonful of the egg whites into the chocolate mixture to loosen it before gently folding in the rest.

■ Put the raspberries into 4 lightly greased ramekins, pour over the chocolate mixture and cook in a preheated oven, at 375°F, for 12–15 minutes, until the souffles have risen.

■ Sprinkle the souffles with confectioners' sugar and serve with extra raspberries, if desired.

CUTS INTO 20

Preparation time 25 minutes
Cooking time 25–30 minutes

INGREDIENTS

1	10 oz white chocolate
2	1 stick butter
3	3 eggs
4	1 teaspoon vanilla extract
5	1 cup chopped dried apricots

PANTRY

¾ cup plus 2 tablespoons superfine sugar; 1⅓ cups all-purpose flour; 2¼ teaspoons baking powder

White Chocolate & Apricot Blondies

■ Break half the chocolate into pieces, put into a saucepan with the butter, and heat gently until melted. Dice the remaining chocolate.

■ Whisk the eggs, sugar, and vanilla extract together in a bowl, using an electric mixer, for about 5 minutes, until thick and foamy and the beaters leave a trail when lifted above the mixture. Fold in the melted chocolate mixture and then the flour and baking powder. Gently fold in half the chopped chocolate and apricots.

■ Pour the mixture into a 7 × 11 inch roasting pan lined with nonstick parchment paper and ease into the corners. Sprinkle with the remaining chocolate and apricots. Bake in a preheated oven, at 350°F, for 25–30 minutes, until it is well risen, the top is crusty, and the center still slightly soft.

■ Let cool in the pan, then lift out using the lining paper and cut into 20 small pieces. Peel off the paper and store in an airtight container for up to 3 days.

CHANGE THE FRUIT

For white chocolate & cranberry blondies, follow the recipe opposite, simply replacing the dried apricots with ½ cup dried cranberries.

MAKES 12

Preparation time 25 minutes, plus cooling
Cooking time 25 minutes

INGREDIENTS

1 18 marshmallows, plus extra chopped pieces to sprinkle

2 1 stick salted butter, softened

3 2 eggs

4 1 teaspoon vanilla extract

5 1¼ cups heavy cream

PANTRY

½ cup superfine sugar; 1¼ cups all-purpose flour; 1¾ teaspoons baking powder

Mile-High Marshmallow Cupcakes

■ Line a 12-cup muffin pan with paper cupcake liners. Cut 8 marshmallows into pieces using kitchen scissors.

■ Put the butter, sugar, eggs, flour, baking powder, and vanilla into a bowl and beat with a handheld electric mixture for about a minute until light and creamy. Stir in the chopped marshmallow pieces and then divide the cake batter among the paper cupcake liners.

■ Bake in a preheated oven, at 350°F, for 20 minutes or until risen and just firm to the touch. Transfer to a wire rack to cool.

■ Cut the remaining marshmallows into small pieces and put about a third in a small saucepan with half the cream. Heat gently until melted. Transfer to a bowl and let cool.

■ Whip the remaining cream in a bowl until just holding its shape. Stir in the marshmallow cream and any remaining marshmallow pieces, then pile onto the cakes. Sprinkle with extra chopped marshmallow pieces to serve.

PRETTY IN PINK

Make the cake batter opposite, but add 1½ cups flaked dried coconut to the bowl with the other cake ingredients, use ¼ cup superfine sugar instead of ½ oz and omit the marshmallows. Bake as opposite. Whip 1 cup heavy cream with 1 tablespoon confectioners' sugar and 2–3 drops of red food coloring until just forming peaks. Pile onto the cooled cakes and sprinkle with extra flaked dried coconut.

SERVES 4-6

Preparation time 15 minutes
Cooking time 15 minutes

INGREDIENTS

1   **6 tablespoons unsalted butter, at room temperature**

2   **3 eggs**

3   **5 tablespoons unsweetened cocoa powder**

PANTRY

⅔ cup firmly packed light brown sugar;
½ cup all-purpose flour; 1 teaspoon baking
powder; 1 cup boiling water; confectioners'
sugar, to decorate

Chocolate Puddle Cake

■ Rub a little of the butter all over the bottom and sides of an ovenproof dish and stand the dish on a baking sheet. Put the butter, ⅓ cup of the lightly packed light brown sugar, and the eggs in a large bowl and sift in the flour, 3 tablespoons cocoa powder, and the baking powder. Beat together until they form a smooth batter. Spoon the batter into the dish and spread the top level.

■ To make a sauce, put the remaining 2 tablespoons cocoa powder and light brown sugar into a small bowl and mix in a little of the measured boiling water to make a smooth paste. Gradually mix in the rest of the water, then pour the cocoa sauce over the batter.

■ Bake in a preheated oven, at 350°F, for 15 minutes or until the sauce has sunk to the bottom of the dish and the cake is well risen.

■ Sift a little confectioners' sugar over the cake. Serve with scoops of vanilla ice cream or a little whipped cream, if desired.

LITTLE CAKES

For individual puddle cakes with orange cream, prepare the batter as opposite and spoon it into 4 lightly greased ramekins. Bake as opposite for 10–12 minutes, until the cakes are well risen. Mix crème fraîche, mascarpone, or Greek yogurt with a little finely grated orange zest and serve with the warm cakes.

Preparation time 10 minutes
Cooking time 7–8 minutes

INGREDIENTS

1 3 tablespoons unsalted butter

2 3 crisp, sweet apples, cored and thickly sliced

3 2 large pinches ground cinnamon

4 4 prepared (8 inch) crepes, made from pancake mix (follow package directions but add extra milk to make a runny batter) or 8 frozen mini panakes or waffles

5 ¼ cup chocolate and hazelnut spread

PANTRY

confectioners' sugar, for dusting

Chocolate Apple Crepes

■ Melt half the butter in a large skillet, then add the apples and cook for 3–4 minutes, stirring and turning until hot and lightly browned. Sprinkle with the cinnamon.

■ Heat the remaining butter in the skillet, add the crepes, and heat for a minute or two on each side to warm the crepes through. Or if using frozen mini pancakes or waffles, prepare them according to the package directions to warm through.

■ Spread a tablespoon of chocolate spread over each crepe, pancake, or waffle. Divide the apples among the crepes, spooning them onto half of each crepe. Fold the uncovered sides over the apples. Alternatively, pile the apple mixture on top of the mini pancakes or waffles.

■ Transfer to shallow plates and dust with sifted confectioners' sugar.

CHANGE THE FRUIT

For peach melba pancakes, cook 2 large, thickly sliced peaches in the butter instead of the apples, omitting the cinnamon. Spread the pancakes with ¼ cup raspberry preserves, then add the peaches and fold. Warm through, then serve sprinkled with fresh raspberries, a dusting of confectioners' sugar, and a scoop of ice cream.

Preparation time 20 minutes, plus chilling
Cooking time 15 minutes

INGREDIENTS

1 1½ sheets chilled store-bought puff pastry

2 1 cup heavy cream

3 ½ vanilla bean

4 7 oz white chocolate, chopped

5 1¼ cups raspberries

PANTRY

a little flour, for dusting; confectioners' sugar, for dusting

White Chocolate & Raspberry Puffs

■ Roll out the pastry dough on a lightly floured surface until ⅛ inch thick. Cut out 6 rectangles, each 5 × 3 inches, and put them on a baking sheet. Chill for 30 minutes. Bake in a preheated oven, at 400°F, for 15 minutes, until the pastry is puffed and golden. Transfer to a wire rack to cool.

■ Put the cream and vanilla bean in a saucepan and heat gently until it reaches boiling point. Remove from the heat and scrape the seeds from the vanilla bean into the cream (discard the bean). Immediately stir in the chocolate and continue stirring until it has melted. Cool, chill for 1 hour, until firm, then beat until spreadable.

■ Split the pastries in half crosswise and fill each with white chocolate cream and raspberries. Serve dusted with sifted confectioners' sugar.

TRY STRAWBERRIES AND CREAM

For strawberry custard creams, make the pastry rectangles opposite then cool. Whip ⅔ cup heavy cream until it forms soft swirls, then fold in ½ cup of store-bought vanilla pudding. Split and fill the pastries with the custard cream and 2 cups sliced strawberries. Dust the tops with sifted confectioners' sugar before serving.

DECADENT TREATS

Preparation time 30 minutes, plus cooling
Cooking time 25 minutes

INGREDIENTS

1 ¾ cup slivered almonds

2 1 stick salted butter, softened

3 1 teaspoon vanilla extract

4 2 eggs

5 6 tablespoons unsalted butter, softened

PANTRY

sunflower oil, for brushing;1¼ cups superfine sugar;
½ cup water; 1¼ cups all-purpose flour; 1¾ teaspoons
baking powder; 1 cup confectioners' sugar;
1 teaspoon hot water

Almond Praline Cupcakes

■ Line a 12-cup muffin pan with paper cupcake liners. Brush a baking sheet lightly with oil. Put ¾ cup of the superfine sugar into a small, heavy saucepan with the water and heat gently until it has dissolved. Bring to a boil and boil rapidly until the syrup has turned to a pale golden caramel. Immediately stir in the slivered almonds. When coated, turn out onto the prepared baking sheet, spread in a thin layer, and let sit until cold and brittle.

■ Snap half the praline into jagged pieces and reserve. Process the remainder in a food processor until ground.

■ Put the salted butter, remaining superfine sugar, vanilla extract, eggs, flour, and baking powder in a bowl and beat with a handheld electric mixer for about a minute until light and creamy. Stir in the ground praline. Divide the cake batter between the paper liners.

■ Bake in a preheated oven, at 350°F, for 20 minutes or until risen and just firm to the touch. Transfer to a wire rack to cool.

■ Beat together the unsalted butter and confectioners' sugar with the hot water in a bowl until pale and creamy. Spread over the cakes using a small spatula. Decorate with the praline pieces.

SERVES 6

Preparation time 10 minutes
Cooking time 10–15 minutes

INGREDIENTS

1 5 small or 3 large nectarines (about 1 lb), pitted and sliced

2 ¼ cup orange liqueur, plus extra to flavor the fruit

3 1½ cups sour cream

4 pinch of freshly grated nutmeg

5 1 teaspoon vanilla extract

PANTRY

⅔ cup firmly packed light brown sugar

Nectarine Brûlée

■ Put the nectarines into a saucepan and add enough water to cover. Poach over low heat for 5–10 minutes, or until tender. Drain and divide among 6 individual ramekins. Stir in a little orange liqueur.

■ Beat together the sour cream, nutmeg, vanilla extract, and the ¼ cup orange liqueur in a bowl until well combined. Spoon the cream over the nectarine slices, then sprinkle the sugar over the top in a thick layer.

■ Cook under a preheated high broiler until the sugar caramelizes. Serve with brandy snaps, amaretti, or lemon cookies.

Preparation time 25 minutes, plus cooling
Cooking time 55 minutes

INGREDIENTS

1 2 teaspoons egg white plus 2 eggs, separated

2 1 cup shelled pistachio nuts

3 2 tablespoons vanilla sugar

4 1 stick salted butter, softened

PANTRY

½ cup superfine sugar; finely grated zest of 1 lemon; ⅔ cup all-purpose flour; ½ teaspoon baking powder; sifted confectioners' sugar, for dusting

Candied Pistachio Cake

■ Whisk the 2 teaspoons egg white in a bowl to break it up. Add the pistachio nuts and coat thinly in the egg white. Sprinkle in the vanilla sugar, turning the nuts to coat, then spread out on a baking sheet lined with parchment paper. Bake in a preheated oven, at 325°F, for 10 minutes. Let cool, then coarsely chop.

■ Beat together the butter, ⅓ cup of the superfine sugar, and the lemon zest in a bowl until pale and fluffy. Beat in the egg yolks. Sift in the flour and baking powder, then stir in the nuts, reserving 3 tablespoons.

■ Whisk the egg whites in a clean bowl with a handheld electric mixer until forming peaks. Gradually whisk in the remaining sugar, a spoonful at a time. Stir a third of the mixture into the creamed mixture using a large metal spoon. Gently stir in the remaining egg whites.

■ Spoon the batter into a greased and lined 9 x 5 x 3 inch or 1¼ quart loaf pan and level the surface. Sprinkle with the reserved nuts and bake in the oven for about 45 minutes or until firm to the touch and a toothpick inserted into the center comes out clean. Loosen the cake at the ends and transfer to a wire rack to cool. Peel off the lining paper and dust with sifted confectioners' sugar.

SERVES 6

Preparation time 25 minutes,
plus soaking and chilling
Cooking time 5 minutes

INGREDIENTS

1 1 envelope or 1 tablespoon
powdered gelatin

2 2 cups rosé wine, plus an extra ⅓ cup

3 8 oz small strawberries,
hulled and halved

4 1 cup heavy cream

PANTRY

¼ cup water; ⅓ cup superfine sugar; finely grated
zest of 1 lemon

Strawberry Rosé Gelatin & Syllabub

■ Spoon the measured water into a small heatproof bowl or mug, then sprinkle the gelatin over the top, tilting the bowl so that the dry powder is completely absorbed by the water. Let soak for 5 minutes.

■ Heat the bowl or mug in a small saucepan of simmering water for 5 minutes or until a clear liquid forms. Remove from the heat, then stir in 3 tablespoons of sugar until dissolved. Cool slightly, then gradually mix into 2 cups rosé wine.

■ Divide the strawberries among 6 tall Champagne-style glasses. Pour the rosé gelatin mixture over the fruit and chill in the refrigerator until the gelatin is set.

■ Mix the lemon zest, remaining sugar, and ⅓ cup wine together to make a syllabub and set aside. When ready to serve, whip the cream until it forms soft swirls, then gradually whisk in the lemon zest mixture. Spoon over the gelatins.

TRY ORANGE & BUBBLES

For for an orange-flavored version,
dissolve the gelatin as opposite,
add 2 tablespoons superfine sugar
and when cool mix in 1 cup blood
(or ordinary) orange juice and
2 cups cheap dry sparkling white
wine. Divide 1¼ cups fresh or frozen
raspberries between the glasses,
then top up with the gelatin. Chill
until set and serve plain.

Preparation time 10 minutes, plus standing,
chilling & freezing
Cooking time 15 minutes

INGREDIENTS

1   1 quart good-quality vanilla ice cream

2   2 cups crushed graham crackers

3   6 tablespoons butter, melted

4   7 oz soft butterscotch fudge

5   2 tablespoons light cream

Caramel Ice Cream Cake

■ Remove the ice cream from the freezer and let stand at room temperature for 30–45 minutes, until it is well softened.

■ Meanwhile, put the crushed cookies into a bowl, add the melted butter and mix together until the cookies are moistened. Press the cookie mixture into a 9 inch round springform pan, pressing it up the edge of the pan to make a 1 inch side. Chill in the refrigerator for 20 minutes.

■ Put the fudge and cream into a saucepan and heat gently, stirring, until the fudge has melted. Carefully spread two-thirds of the fudge mixture over the cookie crust. Spoon the ice cream over the top and level the surface.

■ Drizzle the remaining caramel over the ice cream with a spoon and freeze for 4 hours. Unmold the cake and serve in wedges.

ADD SOME CHOCOLATE

For a chocolate & caramel cake, make the cookie crust opposite, but use 2 cups crushed chocolate cookies. Melt the fudge with the cream as above, then stir in 1¼ cups toasted ground hazelnuts. Pour all the mixture over the cookie crust, then top with the softened vanilla ice cream. Melt 2 oz semisweet chocolate in a heatproof bowl set over a saucepan of gently simmering water (don't let the bowl touch the water). Drizzle it over the ice cream and freeze as opposite.

CUTS INTO 8

Preparation time 15 minutes
Cooking time 40 minutes

INGREDIENTS

1	8 oz semisweet or bittersweet chocolate, broken into pieces
2	1 stick unsalted butter
3	¼ cup heavy cream
4	4 eggs, separated
5	2 tablespoons unsweetened cocoa powder, sifted

PANTRY

⅔ cup superfine sugar

Chocolate Truffle Cake

■ Melt the chocolate, butter, and cream together in a heatproof bowl set over a saucepan of gently simmering water. Remove from the heat and let cool for 5 minutes.

■ Whisk the egg yolks with ⅓ cup of the superfine sugar until pale and stir in the cooled chocolate mixture.

■ Whisk the egg whites in a large clean bowl until forming soft peaks, then whisk in the remaining superfine sugar. Fold into the egg yolk mixture with the sifted cocoa powder until evenly incorporated.

■ Pour the cake batter into an oiled 9 inch spring-form cake pan that has been lined with parchment paper along the bottom and lightly dusted all over with a little extra cocoa powder. Bake in a preheated oven, at 350°F, for 35 minutes.

■ Let cool in the pan for 10 minutes, then turn out onto a serving plate. Serve in wedges, while still warm, with whipped cream and strawberries.

TRY IT WITH ORANGE

For chocolate & brandied orange cake, add the finely grated zest of 1 orange when folding in the confectioners' sugar opposite. Remove and discard the zest from 3 oranges, cut into segments, and soak in 3 tablespoons brandy and 1 tablespoon honey. Serve the oranges with the cake along with crème fraîche or cream.

Preparation time 20 minutes, plus chilling and cooling
Cooking time 45–50 minutes

INGREDIENTS

1 1 (1 lb) package chilled store-bought rolled dough piecrust or enough homemade for a 10 inch pie

2 3 eggs plus 1 egg yolk

3 2 cups heavy cream

PANTRY

½ cup superfine sugar; ⅔ cup lemon juice; confectioners' sugar, for dusting

Classic Lemon Tart

■ Roll out the pie dough thinly on a lightly floured surface and use it to line a 10 inch fluted tart pan. Prick the pastry shell with a fork and then chill in the refrigerator for 15 minutes.

■ Line the pastry shell with nonstick parchment paper, add pie weights or dried beans, and bake in a preheated oven, at 375°F, for 15 minutes. Remove the lining paper and weights and bake for another 10 minutes, until crisp and golden. Remove from the oven and reduce the temperature to 300°F.

■ Beat together the eggs, egg yolk, heavy cream, sugar, and lemon juice, then pour into the pastry shell.

■ Bake for 20–25 minutes or until the filling is just set. Let the tart cool completely, then dust with confectioners' sugar and serve.

MAKE AN ACCOMPANIMENT

For mixed berries with cassis, to serve with the tart, mix 1½ cups sliced hulled strawberries (or halved if small), with 1 cup raspberries, 1 cup blueberries, 3 tablespoons superfine sugar, and 2 tablespoons crème de cassis. Soak for 1 hour before serving.

CUTS INTO 10

Preparation time 15 minutes, plus standing
Cooking time 1¼ hours

INGREDIENTS

1   5 chai tea bags

2   1½ cups mixed dried fruit, such as raisins, golden raisins, cranberries, and/or chopped apricots

3   ⅓ cup Brazil nuts, chopped

4   4 tablespoons butter

5   1 egg, beaten

PANTRY

1¼ cups boiling water; 2 cups all-purpose flour; 1 tablespoon baking powder; ⅔ cup firmly packed light brown sugar

Chai Tea Bread

■ Stir the tea bags into the measured water in a small bowl and let stand for 10 minutes.

■ Grease a 9 x 5 x 3 inch or 1¼ quart loaf pan and line with parchment paper.

■ Mix together the flour, baking powder, sugar, dried fruit, and nuts in a bowl. Remove the tea bags from the water, pressing them against the side of the small bowl to squeeze out all the water. Thinly slice the butter into the water and stir until melted. Let cool slightly. Add to the dry ingredients with the egg and mix together well.

■ Spoon the batter into the prepared pan and spread the mixture into the corners. Bake in a preheated oven, at 325°F, for 1¼ hours or until risen, firm and a toothpick inserted into the center comes out clean.

■ Loosen the cake at the ends and transfer to a wire rack. Peel off the lining paper and let cool. Spread the top with Chai Cream Frosting, if desired (see opposite).

FROST THE CAKE

For chai cream frosting to spread over the cake, put ¼ cup milk and 3 chai tea bags into a saucepan and bring to a boil. Remove from the heat and let the tea bags steep in the milk until cold. Discard the tea bags, squeezing them to extract the liquid. Beat together 1 cup cream cheese and 2 tablespoons soft unsalted butter in a bowl until smooth. Beat in the flavored milk and ⅔ cup confectioners' sugar, sifted.

SERVES 4

Preparation time 15 minutes
Cooking time none

INGREDIENTS

1 1 cup fromage blanc, quark, or thick Greek–style plain yogurt

2 ¾ cup sweetened chestnut spread (available online)

3 8 meringue shells, crushed

4 semisweet chocolate shards cut from a bar, to decorate

PANTRY

1 tablespoon confectioners' sugar, sifted

Sweet Chestnut Meringue Cups

■ Beat the fromage blanc, quark, or yogurt with the confectioners' sugar. Stir in half the chestnut spread and the crushed meringues.

■ Spoon the remaining chestnut spread into individual serving dishes and top with the meringue mixture. Decorate with the chocolate shards and serve.

TRY IT WITH PANCAKES

For sweet chestnut pancakes, stir the chestnut spread into the fromage blanc, quark, or yogurt. Heat 8 frozen mini pancakes according to the package directions and spread them with the chestnut mix. Sprinkle with cocoa powder and confectioners' sugar to serve.

Preparation time 10 minutes
Cooking time 20 minutes

INGREDIENTS

1 1¼ lb semisweet chocolate

2 8 oz milk chocolate

3 1 cup mascarpone cheese

4 ¾ cup raspberries

5 finely chopped nuts, to decorate

Chocolate Millefeuilles

■ Break the semisweet and milk chocolate into pieces, place in separate heatproof bowls, and melt over saucepans of barely simmering water, making sure the water does not touch the surface of the bowls.

■ Spread a thin layer of melted semisweet chocolate onto a sheet of parchment paper. Drizzle melted milk chocolate over the top and feather the 2 chocolates together. Let stand until set but not brittle.

■ Cut into 3 inch squares, then let stand until brittle before peeling away the paper.

■ Layer the chocolate rectangles with spoonfuls of mascarpone and raspberries and sprinkle with some nuts to decorate.

MAKE IT FRUITY

For raspberry millefeuilles, use 1¾ lb white chocolate to make the squares as opposite. Layer with cream and raspberries. Make a raspberry sauce by mixing 1 cup fresh raspberries with 1 teaspoon confectioners' sugar. Press the mixture through a strainer. Drizzle the sauce around the millefeuilles before serving.

SERVES 4

Preparation time 15 minutes, plus cooling
and chilling
Cooking time about 10 minutes

INGREDIENTS

1 ½ cup slivered almonds, toasted

2 ¾ cup coconut milk

3 1¼ cups heavy cream

4 15 cardamom seeds, lightly crushed

PANTRY

½ cup granulated sugar;
2 tablespoons superfine sugar

Coconut Syllabub & Almond Brittle

■ To make the brittle, put the granulated sugar and slivered almonds into a saucepan over low heat. While the sugar melts, lightly oil a baking sheet. When the sugar has melted and turned golden, pour the mixture onto the baking sheet and let cool.

■ To make the syllabub, pour the coconut milk and heavy cream into a large bowl. Add the crushed cardamom seeds and superfine sugar, then lightly whip until just holding soft peaks.

■ Spoon the syllabub into 4 glasses and chill in the refrigerator. Meanwhile, lightly crack the brittle into irregular shards. When ready to serve, top the syllabub with some of the brittle and serve the remainder separately on the side.

Preparation time 8 minutes
Cooking time none

INGREDIENTS

1 6 passion fruit, halved, flesh and seeds removed

2 1¼ cups Greek yogurt

3 1 tablespoon honey

4 1 cup heavy cream, whipped to soft peaks

5 4 pieces of shortbread or vanilla cookies, to serve

Passion Fruit Yogurt Whips

■ Stir the passion fruit flesh and seeds into the yogurt with the honey.

■ Fold the cream into the yogurt. Spoon into tall glasses and serve with the shortbread.

MIX UP THE FRUIT

For mango & lime yogurt whips, omit the passion fruit, instead pureeing 1 large ripe peeled and pitted mango with the zest of 1 lime and confectioners' sugar to taste. Mix into the yogurt and fold in the cream. Omit the honey.

Preparation time 25 minutes
Cooking time 1 hour

INGREDIENTS

1   1 sheet store-bought puff pastry

2   1½ sticks salted butter, softened

3   3 eggs

4   6 figs, quartered

PANTRY

¾ cup plus 2 tablespoons superfine sugar;
1⅔ cups all-purpose flour; 1¾ teaspoons baking
powder; ¾ cup confectioners' sugar, sifted;
1 tablespoon lemon juice

Iced Fig Slice

■ Roll out the pastry on a lightly floured surface and use to line a greased 9 inch square shallow baking pan or small roasting pan. Line the pastry shell with wax paper and fill with pie weights or dried beans. Bake in a preheated oven, at 400°F, for 15 minutes. Remove from the oven and remove the paper and weights. Reduce the oven temperature to 350°F.

■ Beat together the butter, superfine sugar, flour, baking powder, and eggs in a bowl until pale and creamy. Spoon the batter over the pastry crust and level the surface. Arrange the figs over the top. Bake in the oven for about 45 minutes or until risen and golden. Let cool in the pan.

■ Make the icing. Beat together the confectioners' sugar and lemon juice in a bowl to make a smooth, spoonable icing. If necessary, beat in a dash of water or extra lemon juice. Drizzle the icing over the cake, then cut into squares or rectangles.

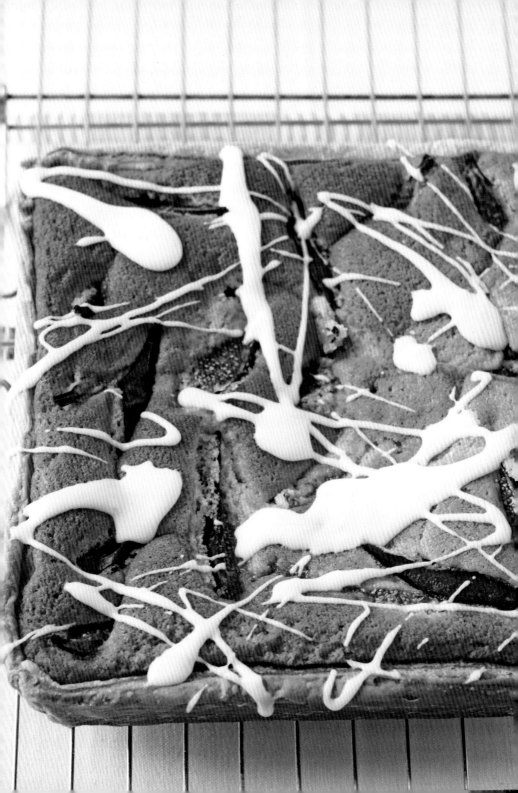

Preparation time 30 minutes
Cooking time 10–12 minutes

INGREDIENTS

1 1 stick butter, diced

2 1 tablespoon lavender petals

3 8 oz strawberries (or a mixture of strawberries and raspberries)

4 ⅔ cup heavy cream

5 16 small lavender flowers (optional)

PANTRY

1¼ cups all-purpose flour; 2½ tablespoons rice flour; ¼ cup superfine sugar; sifted confectioners' sugar, for dusting

Strawberry & Lavender Shortcakes

■ Put the all-purpose flour and rice flour into a mixing bowl or a food processor. Add the butter and rub in with your fingertips or process until the mixture resembles fine bread crumbs.

■ Stir in the sugar and lavender petals and squeeze the crumbs together with your hands to form a smooth ball. Knead lightly then roll out on a lightly floured surface until ¼ inch thick. Stamp out 3 inch circles using a fluted round cookie cutter. Transfer to an ungreased baking sheet. Reknead the scraps and continue rolling and stamping out until you have made 16 cookies.

■ Prick with a fork, bake in a preheated oven, at 325°F, for 10–12 minutes, until pale golden. Let cool on the baking sheet.

■ To serve, halve 4 of the smallest strawberries, hull and slice the rest. Whip the cream and spoon over 8 of the cookies. Top with the sliced strawberries, then the remaining cookies. Spoon the remaining cream on top and decorate with the reserved halved strawberries and tiny sprigs of lavender, if desired. Dust lightly with sifted confectioners' sugar. These are best eaten on the day they are filled, but the plain cookies can be stored in an airtight container for up to 3 days.

MAKES 12

Preparation time 15 minutes
Cooking time 20 minutes

INGREDIENTS

1 1 stick salted butter, softened

2 2 eggs

3 2 teaspoons espresso coffee powder

4 ½ cup slivered almonds, lightly toasted

5 ¼ teaspoon ground cinnamon

PANTRY

⅔ cup superfine sugar, plus 2 teaspoons;
1¼ cups all-purpose flour; 1¾ teaspoons baking
powder; 1 teaspoon boiling water

Marbled Coffee Cupcakes

■ Line a 12-cup muffin pan with paper cupcake liners.

■ Put the butter, ⅔ cup superfine sugar, eggs, flour, and baking powder into a bowl and beat with a handheld electric mixer for about a minute until light and creamy.

■ Spoon half the cake batter into a separate bowl. Blend the coffee powder with a boiling water and stir into half the batter. Using a teaspoon, fill the paper liners with the 2 batters, then draw a knife in a circular motion through each cupcake to mix the batter partly together to create a marbled effect.

■ Sprinkle the slivered almonds over the cakes. Mix the remaining 2 teaspoons sugar with the cinnamon and sprinkle over the cakes.

■ Bake in a preheated oven, at 350°F, for 20 minutes or until risen and just firm to the touch. Transfer to a wire rack to cool.

TRY A FRUITY CUPCAKE

For rippled raspberry cupcakes, make the cake batter as opposite. Crush ⅔ cup fresh raspberries in a bowl with 2 teaspoons superfine sugar so that they are broken up but not turning to a juicy mush. Fill the paper liners halfway with the cake batter and flatten with the back of a spoon. Divide the raspberry mixture among the liners and top with the remaining cake batter. Bake as opposite and serve dusted with confectioners' sugar.

FAMILY FAVORITES

SERVES 4

Preparation time 10 minutes
Cooking time 5 minutes

INGREDIENTS

1 ½ cup store-bought chocolate sauce

2 6 small chocolate chip cookies, broken into small pieces

3 16 small scoops of vanilla ice cream

4 16 pink and white marshmallows, plus a few mini marshmallows, to decorate

5 grated chocolate, to decorate

Rocky Road Ice Cream Sundaes

■ Put the chocolate sauce into a saucepan over low heat and warm through.

■ Meanwhile, place a handful of the cookie pieces into each of 4 tall sundae glasses. Add 2 scoops of vanilla ice cream to each glass. Add 4 of the marshmallows to each sundae, then spoon 1 tablespoon of the warm chocolate sauce over each. Repeat the layers, finishing with the chocolate sauce.

■ Decorate with a few mini marshmallows and a little grated chocolate. Serve immediately with long spoons.

MAKES 8

Preparation time 30 minutes
Cooking time 1–1¼ hours

INGREDIENTS

1	**3 egg whites**
2	**1 small ripe banana**
3	**⅔ cup heavy cream**
4	**½ cup store-bought dulce de leche (caramel sauce)**

PANTRY

½ cup firmly packed light brown sugar;
⅔ cup superfine sugar; 1 tablespoon lemon juice

Banana-Caramel Meringues

■ Whisk the egg whites in a large clean bowl until stiff. Gradually whisk in the sugars, a teaspoonful at a time, until it has all been added. Whisk for another few minutes until the meringue mixture is thick and glossy.

■ Using a tablespoon, take a scoop of meringue mixture, then scoop it off the first spoon by using a second spoon and drop it onto a large baking sheet lined with nonstick parchment paper to make an oval-shape meringue. Continue until all the mixture has been used.

■ Bake in a preheated oven, at 225°F, for 1–1¼ hours or until the meringues are firm and may be easily peeled off the paper. Let cool on the paper.

■ To serve, coarsely mash the banana with the lemon juice. Whip the cream until it forms soft swirls, then whisk in 2 tablespoons of the dulce de leche. Combine with the mashed banana, then use to sandwich the meringues together in pairs and arrange in paper cupcake liners. Drizzle with the remaining caramel sauce and serve immediately. Unfilled meringues may be stored in an airtight container for up to 3 days.

TRY COFFEE CARAMEL

For coffee-caramel meringues, make the meringues opposite. To make the filling, whip the cream, then stir in 1–2 teaspoons instant coffee dissolved in 1 teaspoon boiling water. Use to sandwich the meringues together in pairs. Drizzle dulce de leche (caramel sauce) over the top of the meringues.

Preparation time 20 minutes
Cooking time 2 hours

INGREDIENTS

1 1 stick unsalted butter

2 ¼ cup light corn syrup

3 2 large cooking apples (about 1 lb), cored and peeled

4 2 eggs, beaten

5 grated zest of 1 orange, and 3 tablespoons of the juice

PANTRY

½ cup superfine sugar; 1⅔ cups all-purpose flour; 1½ teaspoons baking powder

Steamed Apple Cake

■ Grease the inside of a deep 1¼ quart round ovenproof dish lightly and line the bottom with a small circle of nonstick parchment paper. Spoon in the syrup, then thickly slice 1 apple and arrange in an even layer on top. Coarsely grate the remaining apple.

■ Cream the butter and sugar in a bowl until pale and creamy. Gradually mix in alternate spoonfuls of beaten egg and flour, adding the baking powder to a spoonful of flour, until all three have been added and the batter is smooth.

■ Stir in the grated apple, orange zest, and juice, then spoon into the prepared dish. Level the surface and cover with a piece of pleated nonstick parchment paper and aluminum foil. Tie in place with string, adding a string handle.

■ Lower the dish into the top of a steamer set over a saucepan of simmering water, cover with a lid, and steam for 2 hours, until the cake is well risen and a knife comes out cleanly when inserted into the center of the sponge.

■ Remove the foil and paper, loosen the edge of the cake, and turn out onto a plate with a rim. Serve immediately.

Preparation time 25 minutes
Cooking time 1 hour–1 hour 10 minutes

INGREDIENTS

1   1½ sticks butter, at room temperature

2   3 eggs, beaten

3   ⅓ cup poppy seeds

4   citron peel, cut into thin strips

PANTRY

¾ cup plus 2 tablespoons superfine sugar;
2 cups all-purpose flour; 1 tablespoon baking
powder; grated zest and juice of 2 lemons;
1 cup confectioners' sugar

Lemon & Poppy Seed Cake

■ Beat the butter and superfine sugar together in a mixing bowl until pale and creamy. Gradually mix in alternate spoonfuls of beaten egg and flour until all has been added and the batter is smooth. Stir in the baking powder, poppy seeds, lemon zest, and 5–6 tablespoons lemon juice to make a soft dropping consistency. Make sure you reserve about 1 tablespoon of lemon juice for the icing.

■ Spoon the batter into a greased 9 x 5 x 3 inch loaf pan, its bottom and 2 long sides also lined with oiled wax paper. Spread the surface level and bake in a preheated oven, at 325°F, for 1 hour–1 hour 10 minutes, until well risen, the top is cracked and golden, and a toothpick inserted into the center comes out clean.

■ Let cool in the pan for 10 minutes, then loosen the edges and lift out of the pan using the lining paper. Transfer to a wire rack, peel off the lining paper, and let cool.

■ Sift the confectioners' sugar into a bowl, then gradually mix in enough of the lemon juice to make a smooth coating of icing. Drizzle over the top of the cake in random squiggly lines. Add strips of citron peel to the top and let set. Store in an airtight container for up to 1 week.

CUTS INTO 8

Preparation time 30 minutes
Cooking time 20 minutes

INGREDIENTS

1   ¾ cup soft margarine

2   3 eggs

3   2 tablespoons instant coffee, dissolved in 1 tablespoon boiling water

4   6 tablespoons butter, at room temperature

5   2 oz semisweet chocolate, melted, for drizzling

PANTRY

¾ cup firmly packjed light brown sugar; 1⅓ cups all-purpose flour; 2¼ teaspoons baking powder; 1¼ cups confectioners' sugar, sifted

Old-Fashioned Coffee Cake

■ Beat together the margarine, brown sugar, flour, baking powder, eggs, and half the dissolved coffee in a mixing bowl or a food processor until smooth.

■ Divide the batter evenly between two 7 inch cake pans, greased and the bottoms lined with oiled wax paper, and spread the surfaces level. Bake in a preheated oven, at 350°F, for 20 minutes, until well risen, the cakes are browned, and they spring back when gently pressed with a fingertip.

■ Let the cakes stand for a few minutes, then loosen the edges, turn out onto a wire rack, and peel off the lining paper. Let cool.

■ Next make the coffee frosting. Put the butter and half the confectioners' sugar into a mixing bowl, add the remaining dissolved coffee, and beat until smooth. Gradually beat in the remaining confectioners' sugar until pale and creamy.

■ Put one of the cakes on a serving plate, spread with half the frosting, then cover with the second cake. Spread the remaining frosting over the top.

■ Pipe or drizzle swirls of melted chocolate on top. This cake can be stored in a cake pan for 2–3 days in a cool place.

MAKES 12

Preparation time 20 minutes
Cooking time 6–9 minutes

INGREDIENTS

1 1 egg, beaten plus 1 egg yolk

2 1 teaspoon vanilla extract

3 1 teaspoon ground cinnamon

PANTRY

1⅔ cups all-purpose flour; ¼ teaspoon salt; ⅓ cup superfine sugar; 1 cup plus 2 tablespoons water; 4 cups sunflower oil

Churros

■ Mix the flour, salt, and 1 tablespoon of the sugar in a bowl. Pour the water into a saucepan and bring to a boil. Remove from the heat, add the flour mixture, and beat well. Then return to the heat and stir until it forms a smooth ball that leaves the sides of the pan almost clean. Remove from the heat and let cool for 10 minutes.

■ Gradually beat the whole egg, egg yolk, then the vanilla extract into the flour mixture until smooth. Spoon into a large nylon pastry bag fitted with a ½ inch wide plain tip.

■ Pour the oil into a medium saucepan to a depth of 1 inch. Heat to 340°F on a candy thermometer or pipe a tiny amount of the batter into the oil. If the oil bubbles instantly, it is ready to use. Pipe coils, S shapes, and squiggly lines into the oil, in small batches, cutting the ends off with kitchen scissors.

Cook the churros for 2–3 minutes, until they float and are golden, turning over, if needed, to brown evenly.

■ Lift the churros out of the oil, drain well on paper towels, then sprinkle with the remaining sugar mixed with the cinnamon. Continue piping and frying until all the batter has been used. Serve warm or cold.

■ These are best eaten on the day they are made.

ADD CITRUS

For orange churros, add the grated zest of 1 orange and omit the vanilla extract. Continue as opposite. Sprinkle with plain superfine sugar when cooked.

Preparation time 40 minutes, plus cooling
Cooking time 30–35 minutes

INGREDIENTS

1 **1 (1 lb) package store-bought rolled dough piecrust or enough homemade for a deep 8-inch piecrust plus the lattice**

2 **6 peaches (about 1½ lb), halved, pitted, and sliced**

3 **1¼ cups raspberries**

4 **milk, to glaze**

PANTRY

⅓ cup superfine sugar, plus extra for sprinkling; 1 teaspoon cornstarch; grated zest of 1 lemon

Peach Melba Pie

■ Reserve one-third of the dough for the lattice. Roll out the remainder on a lightly floured surface until large enough to line the bottom and sides of a buttered metal pie plate, 8 inches in diameter and 2 inches deep. Lift the dough over a rolling pin, drape into the pie plated, then press over the bottom and sides.

■ Mix the sugar, cornstarch, and lemon zest together, then add the fruits and toss together gently. Pile into the pie plate. Trim off the excess dough, add to the reserved portion, then roll out. Cut into ¾ inch wide strips long enough to go over the top of the pie.

■ Brush the top edge of the pie shell with milk and arrange the dough strips over the top as a lattice. Trim off the excess. Brush with milk, then sprinkle with a little sugar.

■ Bake in a preheated oven, at 375°F, for 30–35 minutes, until golden. Let cool for 15 minutes, then serve cut into wedges and drizzled with melba sauce (see opposite).

A SAUCEY EXTRA

For melba sauce to serve as an accompaniment, put 1⅔ cups raspberries in a saucepan with the juice of ½ lemon and 2 tablespoons confectioners' sugar, and cook for 2–3 minutes, until the raspberries are just tender. Cool, then puree in a blender and strain to remove the seeds. Serve warm or cold.

Preparation time 15 minutes
Cooking time 16–20 minutes

INGREDIENTS

1 ½ teaspoon ground cinnamon

2 ½ teaspoon ground ginger

3 ¼ teaspoon ground allspice

4 4 tablespoons butter, diced

5 2 tablespoons light corn syrup

PANTRY

¾ cup all-purpose flour; 1 teaspoon baking powder; ½ teaspoon baking soda; finely grated zest of 1 lemon; ¼ cup superfine sugar

Spiced Cookies

■ Mix together the flour, baking powder, baking soda, spices, and lemon zest in a mixing bowl.

■ Add the butter and rub in with your fingertips until the mixture resembles fine bread crumbs.

■ Stir in the sugar, add the syrup, and mix first with a spoon, then squeeze the crumbs together with your hands to form a ball.

■ Shape the dough into a log, then slice into 12 disks. Roll each piece into a ball and arrange on 2 large greased baking sheets, leaving space between for them to spread during cooking.

■ Cook one baking sheet at a time in the center of a preheated oven, at 350°F, for 8–10 minutes or until the cookie tops are cracked and golden.

■ Let the cookies harden for 1–2 minutes, then loosen and transfer to a wire rack to cool completely. Store in an airtight container for up to 3 days.

SERVES 4

Preparation time 15 minutes, plus freezing time
Cooking time 5 minutes

INGREDIENTS

1   4 slices jellyroll cakes or 4 individual sponge cake shells

2   4 scoops strawberry and vanilla ice cream or vanilla ice cream

3   2 egg whites

4   1½ cups frozen mixed summer fruits, such as raspberries, blackerries, blueberries, red currants, and/or halved or quartered hulled strawberries, just defrosted or warmed in a small saucepan

PANTRY

¼ cup superfine sugar

Mini Baked Alaskas

■ Arrange the slices of jellyroll cake or sponge cakes, well spaced apart, on a baking sheet, then top each with a scoop of ice cream. Put into the freezer for 10 minutes (or longer if you have time).

■ Whisk the egg whites in a large bowl until stiff, moist-looking peaks form. Gradually whisk in the sugar, a teaspoon at a time, and continue whisking for a few minutes, until thick and glossy.

■ Remove the cake and ice cream from the freezer and quickly swirl the meringue over the top and sides to cover completely. Cook in a preheated oven, at 400°F, for 5 minutes, until the peaks are golden brown, the meringue is cooked through, and the ice cream is only just beginning to soften.

■ Transfer the baked Alaskas to shallow serving bowls and spoon the mixed fruit around the desserts. Serve immediately.

MAKES 32

Preparation time 10 minutes
Cooking time 12 minutes

INGREDIENTS

1 1 stick unsalted butter, at room temperature

2 ½ cup chunky peanut butter

3 1 egg, lightly beaten

4 1 cup unsalted peanuts

PANTRY

⅔ cup firmly packed light brown sugar; 1¼ cups all-purpose flour; ½ teaspoon baking powder

Peanut Butter Cookies

■ Beat the butter and sugar together in a mixing bowl or a food processor until pale and creamy. Add the peanut butter, egg, flour, and baking powder and stir together until combined. Stir in the peanuts.

■ Drop large teaspoonfuls of the dough onto 3 large, lightly oiled baking sheets, leaving 2 inch gaps between each for them to spread during cooking.

■ Flatten the mounds slightly and bake in a preheated oven, at 375°F, for 12 minutes, until golden around the edges. Let cool on the baking sheets for 2 minutes, then transfer to a wire rack to cool completely.

ADD CHOCOLATE CHIPS

For peanut butter & chocolate chip cookies, use only ⅓ cup unsalted peanuts and add ¼ cup milk chocolate chips. Then make and bake the cookies as opposite.

Preparation time 7 minutes
Cooking time 15 minutes

INGREDIENTS

1 5 Granny Smith apples (about 2 lb), peeled, cored, and thickly sliced

2 6 tablespoons butter

3 1⅔ cups fresh whole wheat bread crumbs

4 3 tablespoons pumpkin seeds

PANTRY

2 tablespoons superfine sugar; 1 tablespoon lemon juice; 2 tablespoons water; 2 tablespoons packed brown sugar

Instant Apple Crisps

■ Put the apples into a saucepan with 2 tablespoons of the butter, the superfine sugar, lemon juice, and measured water. Cover and simmer for 8–10 minutes, until softened.

■ Make a crumb topping by melting the remaining butter in a skillet, add the bread crumbs, and cook, stirring, until lightly golden, then add the pumpkin seeds and cook, stirring, for another 1 minute. Remove from the heat and stir in the brown sugar.

■ Spoon the apple mixture into bowls, sprinkle with the crumb topping, and serve.

CHANGE THE FRUIT

For instant pear & chocolate crisps, cook 4 pears (2 lb) in the butter, sugar, and water as in the recipe opposite, adding ½ teaspoon ground ginger to the butter. Prepare the crumb topping opposite, replacing the pumpkin seeds with 2 oz coarsely chopped semisweet chocolate. Cook as opposite.

Preparation time 20 minutes
Cooking time 20 minutes

INGREDIENTS

1 8 ladyfingers or 4 individual plain sponge cakes

2 3 tablespoons orange juice

3 3 cups frozen mixed berries, such as raspberries, blueberries, blackberries and halved or quarted hulled strawberries, just thawed

4 1¾ cups store-bought vanilla pudding

5 3 egg whites

PANTRY

⅓ cup granulated sugar

Warm Summer Fruit Trifle

■ Crumble the ladyfingers or cakes into the bottom of 6 individual ovenproof dishes. Drizzle the orange juice over the tops, then add the mixed fruits. Dollop the vanilla pudding over the tops.

■ Whisk the egg whites in a clean, dry bowl until stiff peaks form, then gradually whisk in the sugar, a spoonful at a time, until all the sugar has been added. Keep whisking for another 1–2 minutes, until the mixture is thick and glossy.

■ Spoon the meringue mixture over the top of the pudding in large swirls. Place the dishes on a baking sheet. Cook in a preheated oven, at 325°F, for 20 minutes, until the meringue is golden brown on top. Serve warm.

MAKE IT SUMMERY

For chilled summer fruit trifle, in the bottom of a large bowl, sprinkle the crumbled ladyfingers or cakes with 3 tablespoons sherry. Top with the thawed fruits, then the vanilla pudding. Whip ⅔ cup heavy cream until it forms soft swirls. Spoon over the top of the trifle instead of the meringue. Chill until ready to serve, then decorate with sugar sprinkles or 4 teaspoons toasted slivered almonds.

SERVES 6

Preparation time 40 minutes, plus chilling and standing
Cooking time 35–40 minutes

INGREDIENTS

 1 sheet chilled store-bought rolled dough piecrust or homemade pie dough for an 8 inch pie

 **4 eggs, separated**

PANTRY

a little flour, for dusting, 1 cup superfine sugar, ⅓ cup cornstarch; grated zest and juice of 2 lemons; ¾–1 cup water

Lemon Meringue Pie

■ Roll out the dough thinly on a lightly floured surface and use to line an 8 inch diameter, 2 inch deep loose-bottom fluted tart pan, pressing evenly into the sides. Trim the top and prick the bottom. Chill for 15 minutes, then line with nonstick parchment paper, add pie weights or dried beans, and bake in a preheated oven, at 375°F, for 15 minutes. Remove the paper and weights and bake for another 5 minutes.

■ Put ⅓ cup of the sugar in a bowl with the cornstarch and lemon zest, add the egg yolks, and mix until smooth. Make the lemon juice up to 1¼ cups with water, pour into a saucepan, and bring to a boil. Gradually mix into the yolk mixture, whisking until smooth. Pour back into the pan and bring to a boil, whisking until thick. Pour into the pastry shell and spread level.

■ Whisk the egg whites until they form stiff peaks. Gradually whisk in the remaining sugar, a teaspoonful at a time, then whisk for another 1–2 minutes, until thick and glossy. Spoon the meringue over the lemon layer to cover completely and swirl with a spoon.

■ Reduce the oven temperature to 350°F and cook for 15–20 minutes, until the meringue is golden and cooked through. Let stand for 15 minutes, then remove the tart pan and transfer to a serving plate. Serve warm or cold.

ADD MORE CITRUS

For citrus meringue pie, mix the grated zest of 1 lime, 1 lemon, and ½ small orange with the cornstarch. Squeeze the juice from the fruits and make up to 1¼ cups with water. Continue as opposite.

Preparation time 15 minutes
Cooking time 1¼ hours

INGREDIENTS

1   ⅓ cup fresh raspberries, plus extra
to serve (optional)

2   2 tablespoons raspberry perserves

3   4 egg whites

PANTRY

1 cup superfine sugar

Raspberry Ripple Meringues

■ Put the raspberries into a bowl and mash with a fork until broken up and turning juicy. Add the preserves and mash together to make a puree. Transfer to a strainer resting over a small bowl and press the puree with the back of a spoon to extract as much juice as possible.

■ Whisk the egg whites in a large clean bowl with a handheld electric mixer until forming peaks. Whisk in a tablespoonful of the sugar and continue to whisk for about 15 seconds. Gradually add the remaining sugar, a spoonful at a time, until thick and glossy.

■ Drizzle the raspberry puree over the meringue and lightly stir in, using a spatula or large metal spoon, scooping up the meringue from the bottom of the bowl so that the mixture is streaked with the puree. Be careful to avoid overmixing.

■ Drop large spoonfuls of the mixture, each about the size of a small orange, onto a large baking sheet lined with parchment paper, then swirl with the back of a teaspoon. Bake in a preheated oven, at 250°F, for about 1¼ hours or until the meringues are crisp and come away easily from the paper. Let cool on the paper. Serve with extra raspberries, if desired.

CUTS INTO 15

Preparation time 20 minutes
Cooking time 35 minutes

INGREDIENTS

 13 oz semisweet chocolate

2 1½ sticks salted butter

3 3 eggs

PANTRY

1 cup firmly packed light brown sugar; ¾ cup all-purpose flour; ¾ teaspoon baking powder

Rich Chocolate Brownies

■ Chop 5 oz of the chocolate into ¼ inch pieces. Break the remaining chocolate into pieces and put in a heatproof bowl with the butter. Melt over a saucepan of gently simmering water (don't let the bottom of the bowl touch the water).

■ Beat the eggs and sugar in a separate bowl until light and foamy. Stir in the melted chocolate mixture. Add the flour, baking powder, and chopped chocolate and mix together until just combined.

■ Spoon the batter into a greased and lined 11 × 7 inch shallow baking pan or roasting pan and level the surface. Bake in a preheated oven, at 375°F), for about 30 minutes or until a crust has formed but the mixture feels soft underneath. Let cool in the pan, then transfer to a board and cut into small squares. Peel off the lining paper.

Preparation time 5 minutes
Cooking time none

FIVE INGREDIENTS

1   3¼ cups frozen mixed summer berries, such as raspberries, blackberries, blueberries, red currants, and/or quartered hulled strawberries

2   1 cup fat-free Greek yogurt

3   wafers or other thin cookies, to serve (optional)

PANTRY

2 tablespoons confectioners' sugar

Frozen Berry Yogurt Ice Cream

■ Put half the berries, the yogurt, and confectioners' sugar into a food processor or blender and blend until fairly smooth and the berries have broken up.

■ Add the rest of the berries and pulse until they are slightly broken up but some texture remains.

■ Place scoops of the yogurt ice cream into bowls and serve immediately with wafers or other cookies, if desired.

TRY IT IN A SUNDAE

Put 1¼ cups raspberries and 1 tablespoon confectioners' sugar into a food processor or blender and blend to make a smooth sauce, then strain to remove the seeds. Make the yogurt ice cream opposite. Break up 4 meringue shells and divide half among 4 glasses. Add 1 scoop of the yogurt ice cream to each glass, then pour over a little of the sauces. Repeat the layers, finishing with the sauce. Serve immediately.

CUTS INTO 10
....
Preparation time 20 minutes, plus cooling
Cooking time 1 hour 25 minutes

INGREDIENTS
....

1 1¾ cups pitted dates, coarsely chopped

....

2 2 small ripe bananas

....

3 1¼ sticks salted butter, softened

....

4 2 eggs

....

5 ½ cup milk

PANTRY
....

finely grated zest and juice of 1 lemon; ½ cup water; ¾ cup superfine sugar; 2¼ cups all-purpose flour; 1 tablespoon baking powder

Date & Banana Ripple Slice

■ Put 1¼ cups of the dates into a small saucepan with the lemon zest and juice and measured water. Bring to a boil, then reduce the heat and simmer gently for 5 minutes, until the dates are soft and pulpy. Mash the mixture with a fork until fairly smooth. Let cool.

■ Grease a 9 x 5 x 3 inch or 1½ quart loaf pan and line the bottom and sides with nonstick parchment paper.

■ Mash the bananas to a puree in a bowl, then add the butter, sugar, eggs, milk, flour, and baking powder and beat together until smooth.

■ Spoon one-third of the batter into the prepared pan and level the surface. Spoon over half the date puree and spread evenly. Add half the remaining cake batter and spread with the remaining puree. Add the remaining cake batter and level the surface.

■ Sprinkle with the reserved dates and bake in a preheated oven, at 325°F, for about 1 hour 20 minutes or until risen and a toothpick inserted into the center comes out clean. Let cool in the pan for 15 minutes, then loosen at the ends and transfer to a wire rack. Peel off the lining paper and let the cake cool completely.

MINI BITES

MAKES 24

Preparation time 30 minutes,
plus chilling and cooling
Cooking time 11–13 minutes

INGREDIENTS

1   **2 sheets chilled store-bought rolled dough piecrust or enough homemade pie dough for 2 small pies**

2   **2 cups blueberries**

3   **milk, to glaze**

PANTRY

2 teaspoons cornstarch; 1 tablespoon water;
3 tablespoons superfine sugar, plus extra for
sprinkling

Blueberry Tarts

■ Roll the dough out thinly on a lightly floured surface, then stamp out twenty-four 2½ inch circles with a fluted cookie cutter and press into the buttered cups of two 12-cup mini muffin pans, reserving any scraps. Prick the bottom of each tart 2–3 times with a fork, then chill for 15 minutes.

■ Meanwhile, mix the cornstarch and measured water to a paste in a saucepan, then add the sugar and half the blueberries. Cook over medium heat for 2–3 minutes, until the blueberries soften and the juices begin to run. Remove from the heat and add the remaining blueberries. Let cool.

■ Roll out the remaining dough scraps and cut out 24 tiny heart shapes. Place the heart shapes on a baking sheet, brush with milk, and sprinkle with superfine sugar.

■ Line the tarts with small squares of nonstick parchment paper and pie weights or dried beans and bake in a preheated oven, at 375°F, for 5 minutes. Remove the paper and weights from the tarts and cook for another 4–5 minutes, until the bottoms are crisp, cooking the heart shapes for 4–5 minutes on the shelf below.

■ Transfer the tart shells to a wire rack to cool. When ready to serve, spoon in the blueberry compote and top with the heart shapes.

MAKES 24

Preparation time 15 minutes
Cooking time 8 minutes

INGREDIENTS

1 ¾ cup sweetened dried coconut, plus 3 tablespoons for sprinkling

2 ¼ cup white chocolate chips

3 ⅔ cup vanilla yogurt

4 1 egg

5 3 tablespoons strawberry preserves, jelly, or jam

PANTRY

1¼ cups all-purpose flour; ½ teaspoon baking soda; 1 teaspoon baking powder; ⅓ cup superfine sugar; ¼ cup sunflower oil

White Chocolate Coconut Muffins

■ Line two 12-section mini muffin pans with paper liners.

■ Sift the flour, baking soda, and baking powder into a bowl and add the sugar, coconut, and white chocolate chips.

■ Mix the yogurt, egg, and sunflower oil together and add to the dry ingredients. Using a large metal spoon, stir the ingredients together until just combined. Divide among the paper liners.

■ Bake in a preheated oven, at 375°F, for 6–8 minutes, until the muffins are well risen and firm. Transfer to a wire rack.

■ Brush with the strawberry preserves, jelly, or jam while the muffins are still warm, and sprinkle with the remaining coconut.

MAKES 12

Preparation time 20 minutes, plus cooling
Cooking time 20–25 minutes

INGREDIENTS

1	1¼ sticks salted butter, softened
2	3 eggs
3	1 teaspoon vanilla extract
4	4 passion fruit
5	⅔ cup heavy cream

PANTRY

¾ cup superfine sugar; 1¼ cups all-purpose flour; 1¾ teaspoons baking powder; ¾–1¼ cups confectioners' sugar, plus 1 tablespoon

Passion Fruit Cream Cupcakes

■ Line a 12-cup muffin pan with paper muffin liners. Put the butter, superfine sugar, eggs, flour, baking powder, and vanilla extract into a bowl and beat with a handheld electric mixer for about a minute until light and creamy. Divide the batter among the paper liners.

■ Bake in a preheated oven, at 350°F, for 20–25 minutes or until risen and just firm to the touch. Transfer to a wire rack to cool.

■ Halve 2 of the passion fruit and scoop the pulp into a bowl with the cream and 1 tablespoon of the confectioners' sugar. Whip until the cream only just holds its shape.

■ Peel away the liners from the cakes and split each cake in half horizontally. Sandwich the halves together with the passion fruit cream.

■ Scoop the pulp from the remaining 2 passion fruit into a bowl. Gradually beat in the remaining confectioners' sugar until you have a thin icing and spread it over the cakes.

CHANGE THE FRUITS

For peach & orange cupcakes, make and bake the cakes as opposite. Let cool and split horizontally. Whip ⅔ cup heavy cream with 1 tablespoon orange-flavored liqueur or orange juice and spoon over the bottom halves of the cakes. Pile 2 thinly sliced pitted ripe peaches on top, then add the lids. Dust generously with confectioners' sugar.

MAKES 16

Preparation time 15 minutes, plus cooling
Cooking time 10 minutes

INGREDIENTS

1   **8 amaretti cookies**

2   **5 tablespoons salted butter, softened**

3   **1 egg**

4   **4 plums, pitted and chopped**

5   **8 unblanched almonds, chopped**

PANTRY

3 tablespoons packed light brown sugar; ½ cup all-purpose flour; 1 teaspoon baking powder; ⅓ cup confectioners' sugar, sifted; 2 teaspoons lemon juice

Amaretti Plum Cakes

■ Place 16 mini silicone muffin cups on a baking sheet.

■ Put the cookies in a plastic bag and crush with a rolling pin until finely ground. Transfer to a bowl and add the sugar, butter, and egg, then sift in the flour and baking powder. Beat with a handheld electric mixer until smooth and creamy. Divide among the cups.

■ Bake in a preheated oven, at 350°F, for 10 minutes, or until risen and just firm. Let rest in the cups for 2 minutes, then transfer to a wire rack to cool completely.

■ Make the icing by beating the confectioners' sugar with the lemon juice to make a smooth paste. Spread a little over the cakes and sprinkle over pieces of the chopped plums and almonds. Drizzle a little more icing on top.

TRY A GINGER VERSION

For apricot & ginger cakes, make the cakes as opposite, using crushed gingersnaps instead of the amaretti and adding 1 finely chopped piece of preserved ginger in syrup. Use small apricots instead of the plums. After baking, drizzle the cakes with some of the ginger syrup instead of the icing.

SERVES 4

Preparation time 15 minutes
Cooking time 20–25 minutes

INGREDIENTS

1 2 sheets ready-rolled puff pastry, defrosted if frozen

2 4 oz marzipan

3 12 canned apricot halves, drained

4 apricot preserves, warmed, to glaze

PANTRY

light brown sugar, for sprinkling

Apricot Tartlets

■ Cut 4 circles from the pastry, using a saucer as a template, each about 3½ inches in diameter. Score a line about ½ inch from the edge of each circle with a sharp knife.

■ Roll out the marzipan to ¼ inch thick and cut out 4 disks to fit inside the scored circles. Lay the pastry circles on a baking sheet, place a disk of marzipan in the center of each, and arrange 3 apricot halves, cut side up, on top. Sprinkle a little sugar into each apricot.

■ Put the baking sheet on top of a second preheated baking sheet (this helps to make the pastry crisp) and bake in a preheated oven, at 400°F, for 20–25 minutes, until the pastry is puffed and browned and the apricots are slightly caramelized around the edges. While still hot, brush the tops with apricot preserves to glaze, then serve.

A JAMAICAN FLAVOR

For banana tartlets with rum mascarpone, follow the recipe opposite, but use 2 thickly sliced bananas in place of the apricots. While the tartlets are baking, in a bowl, mix together ¼ cup mascarpone cheese, 2 tablespoons rum, and 2 tablespoons packed light brown sugar. Spoon on top of the hot tartlets, then serve.

MAKES 12

Preparation time 30 minutes
Cooking time 35–40 minutes

INGREDIENTS

1   1 (1 lb) package store-bought puff pastry

2   3 eggs plus 2 egg yolks

3   1 teaspoon vanilla extract

4   1¼ cups light cream

PANTRY

1 tablespoon vanilla sugar; ⅓ cup superfine sugar; sifted confectioners' sugar, for dusting

Mini Custard Tarts

■ Roll out the pastry on a floured surface to ¼ inch thick. Cut in half and sprinkle one half with the vanilla sugar. Lay the second piece on top and thinly roll out the pastry. Cut out 12 circles using a 3¾ inch plain cookie cutter. Reroll the scraps to make more circles.

■ Press the circles into the cups of a 12-cup nonstick muffin pan, pressing firmly into the cups. Line the pastry shells with squares of aluminum foil. (To do this, wrap each foil square tightly around half a lemon, then remove. Press the foil domes firmly into the pastry shells.)

■ Bake in a preheated oven, at 400°F, for 15 minutes. Remove the foil and bake the shells for another 5 minutes, until crisp. Reduce the oven temperature to 325°F.

■ Meanwhile, beat together the eggs, egg yolks, superfine sugar, and vanilla in a heatproof bowl. Bring the cream to a boil in a saucepan and pour it over the egg mixture, whisking well. Strain into a small bowl and pour into the shells. Bake in the oven for 15–20 minutes or until just set and still slightly wobbly in the center. Let cool in the pan. Serve dusted with sifted confectioners' sugar.

SWEET LEMON TARTS

For sweet lemon tarts, make and bake the pastry shells as opposite, omitting the vanilla sugar. Heat 1⅔ cups light corn syrup in a saucepan until slightly thinned. Remove from the heat and beat in 1⅔ cups fresh white bread crumbs, the finely grated zest of 2 lemons, and 3 tablespoons lemon juice. Cool slightly, then beat in 1 egg and 1 egg yolk. Divide among the liners and return to the oven for 15 minutes, until lightly set.

MAKES 12

Preparation time 15 minutes
Cooking time 25 minutes

INGREDIENTS

1	1 stick salted butter, softened
2	2 eggs
3	1 teaspoon vanilla extract
4	1 cup pecans, coarsely chopped
5	1 cup dulce de leche (caramel sauce)

PANTRY

½ cup firmly packed light brown sugar; 1¼ cups all-purpose flour; 1¾ teaspoons baking powder

Warm Pecan Caramel Cupcakes

■ Line a 12-cup muffin pan with paper cupcake liners. Put the butter, sugar, eggs, flour, baking powder, and vanilla extract into a bowl and beat with a handheld electric mixer for about a minute until light and creamy.

■ Stir in three-quarters of the pecans, then divide the batter among the paper liners.

■ Bake in a preheated oven, at 350°F, for 20 minutes or until risen and just firm to the touch. Transfer to a wire rack.

■ Put the caramel sauce into a small saucepan and stir gently over medium heat until melted but not boiling. Drizzle the sauce over the cakes while still warm and sprinkle with the remaining nuts. You may want to take the cakes out of their paper liners to serve.

Preparation time 25 minutes, plus cooling
Cooking time 12 minutes

INGREDIENTS

1 5 tablespoons salted butter, softened

2 1 teaspoon vanilla extract

3 1 egg

4 6 tablespoons unsalted butter, softened

5 pink food coloring

PANTRY

⅓ cup superfine sugar; ½ cup all-purpose flour,
sifted with ½ teaspoon baking powder; ¾ cup
confectioners' sugar, sifted, plus extra for dusting;
1 teaspoon hot water

Baby Butterflies

■ Place 16 mini silicone muffin cups on
a baking sheet.

■ Put the salted butter, superfine sugar,
flour and baking powder mixture, vanilla
extract, and egg into a bowl and beat with
a handheld electric mixer until light and
creamy. Divide among the cups.

■ Bake in a preheated oven, at 350°F, for
10–12 minutes, until risen and just firm. Let
cool in the cups for 2 minutes, then transfer
to a wire rack to cool completely.

■ Make the buttercream by beating
together the unsalted butter and
confectioners' sugar until combined. Add a
little pink food coloring and the measured
water and beat until smooth and creamy.

■ Use a small, sharp knife to cut out circles
from the tops of the cakes and cut the
circles in half to shape butterfly wings.

■ Put the buttercream into a pastry bag
fitted with a small star tip and use to pipe
swirls into the scooped-out tops of the
cakes. Position the butterfly wings on top
and dust lightly with confectioners' sugar.

ADD A FROSTING

For white chocolate frosting, melt 3½ oz chopped white chocolate with 2 tablespoons unsalted butter in a microwave until no lumps remain. Remove from the heat and sift in ¾ cup confectioners' sugar. Stir well until combined. Use instead of the buttercream to spoon or pipe onto the cupcakes.

MAKES 16

Preparation time 15 minutes, plus cooling
Cooking time 20 minutes

INGREDIENTS

1 | 1 ¾ sticks unsalted butter softened

2 | 1 teaspoon vanilla extract

3 | 3 tablespoons raspberry or strawberry preserves, jelly, or jam

PANTRY

¼ cup superfine sugar; 2 cups all-purpose flour, sifted; vanilla sugar, for sprinkling

Viennese Whirls

■ Place 16 mini silicone muffin cups on a baking sheet.

■ Beat together the butter and superfine sugar until pale and creamy. Beat in the flour and vanilla extract until smooth. Put into a pastry bag fitted with a ½ inch star tip. Pipe a little mixture into the bottom of each cup. Pipe a ring of the mixture on top to create nest shapes.

■ Bake in a preheated oven, at 350°F, for 15–20 minutes, until pale golden. Let stand in the cups for 5 minutes, then transfer to a wire rack. Impress holes into the centers of the nests if they have expanded during cooking. Let cool.

■ Place a little preserves, jelly, or jam in the center of each nest and sprinkle vanilla sugar over the edges.

MAKE THEM CHOCOLATY

For chocolate thumbprint cookies, make the cookie mixture opposite, replacing 3 tablespoons of the flour with 3 tablespoons unsweetened cocoa powder. Spoon the dough into the cups and push a hole into the center of each, using your thumb. Bake as opposite and let cool. Put ⅓ cup chocolate hazelnut spread into a pastry bag fitted with a small star tip and pipe a swirl into the center of each.

Preparation time 15 minutes
Cooking time 12 minutes

INGREDIENTS

1   **10 cardamom pods**

2   **2 egg whites**

3   **½ teaspoon hot chili powder**

4   **¾ cup ground almonds**

PANTRY

2 teaspoons cornstarch; ⅔ cup superfine sugar

Chili & Cardamom Morsels

■ Grease and line a large baking sheet with nonstick parchment paper.

■ Crush the cardamom pods, using a mortar and pestle to release the seeds. Remove the shells and crush the seeds until fairly finely ground.

■ Whisk the egg whites in a thoroughly clean bowl until forming peaks. Sift the cornstarch and chili powder into the bowl and sprinkle in the crushed cardamom. Add the sugar and ground almonds and gently fold the ingredients together to make a sticky paste.

■ Put into a pastry bag fitted with a ½ inch plain tip and pipe oblongs, 2 inches long, onto the baking sheet, spacing them slightly apart.

■ Bake in a preheated oven, at 350°F, for 10–12 minutes, until crisp and pale golden. Transfer to a wire rack to cool.

A MILDER COOKIE

For hazelnut & orange cookies, blend ¾ cup blanched hazelnuts in a food processor or blender until ground. Make the oblongs opposite, omitting the spices and adding the finely grated zest of 1 small orange with the superfine sugar and adding the hazelnuts instead of the ground almonds.

MAKES 16

Preparation time 15 minutes, plus soaking
Cooking time 12 minutes

INGREDIENTS

1 ⅓ **cup raisins**

2 ¼ **cup marsala**

3 **1 teaspoon instant espresso coffee powder, plus an extra ½ teaspoon**

4 ½ **cup plain yogurt**

5 **1 egg, beaten**

PANTRY

2 teaspoons boiling water; 1 cup all-purpose flour; 1½ teaspoons baking powder; ⅓ cup superfine sugar; 2 tablespoons vegetable oil; 1½ teaspoons hot water; ⅓ cup confectioners' sugar

Marsala, Raisin & Coffee Muffins

■ Put the raisins and marsala into a small saucepan and heat until hot but not boiling. Pour into a bowl and let stand for 2 hours, until the raisins have plumped up.

■ Place 16 mini silicone muffin cups on a baking sheet.

■ Mix 1 teaspoon coffee powder with the 2 teaspoons boiling water. Sift the flour and baking powder into a bowl. Stir in the superfine sugar.

■ Mix together the yogurt, egg, oil, and coffee mixture and stir in the raisins and any unabsorbed liquid. Add to the dry ingredients. Using a large metal spoon, stir the ingredients together until only just combined. Divide among the cups.

■ Bake in a preheated oven, at 400°F, for about 12 minutes, until risen and firm. Let stand in the cups for 2 minutes, then transfer to a wire rack to cool.

■ Make the icing by mixing the remaining espresso coffee powder in a small bowl with the hot water until blended. Sift over the confectioners' sugar, beat again, then drizzle over the muffins.

MAKE IT MOCHA

For mocha cream muffins, make the muffins opposite, omitting the raisins and red wine and replacing them with 2 oz chopped white chocolate and 1 tablespoon unsweetened cocoa powder. After baking, mix together 2 teaspoons superfine sugar, ½ teaspoon ground cinnamon, and ½ teaspoon unsweetened cocoa powder and use to sprinkle generously over the muffins.

Preparation time 20 minutes, plus standing
Cooking time 15 minutes

INGREDIENTS

1   **butter, for greasing**

2   **⅔ cup ground almonds**

3   **2 egg whites**

4   **pink and green food coloring**

PANTRY

⅓ cup confectioners' sugar, ½ cup superfine sugar

French Macarons

■ Grease and line 2 baking sheets with nonstick parchment paper.

■ Put the confectioners' sugar into a food processor with the ground almonds and blend to a fine consistency.

■ Put the egg whites in a thoroughly clean bowl and whisk until forming stiff peaks. Gradually whisk in the superfine sugar, a tablespoonful at a time, and whisking well after each addition, until thick and glossy. Divide the mixture equally between 2 bowls and add a few drops of food coloring to each bowl. Divide the almond mixture equally between the 2 bowls and use a metal spoon to stir the mixtures gently to combine.

■ Place 1 color in a pastry bag fitted with a ½ inch plain tip and pipe twelve 1¼ inch circles onto 1 baking sheet. Tap the baking

sheet firmly to smooth the surfaces of the macarons. Wash and dry the pastry bag and piping tip and pipe 12 circles in the second color onto the other baking sheet. Let stand for 30 minutes.

■ Bake in a preheated oven, at 325°F, for about 15 minutes, or until the surfaces feel crisp. Let cool before carefully peeling away the paper.

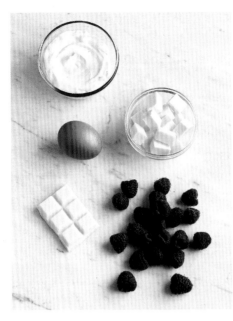

MAKES 16

Preparation time 25 minutes, plus cooling
Cooking time 12 minutes

INGREDIENTS

| 1 | 5 tablespoons salted butter, softened |

| 2 | 1 egg |

| 3 | 1½ oz white chocolate, chopped into small pieces, plus chocolate curls, to decorate |

| 4 | ⅔ cup raspberries |

| 5 | ⅔ cup cream cheese cheese |

PANTRY

3 tablespoons superfine sugar; ½ cup all-purpose flour; ½ teaspoon baking powder; 1 tablespoon confectioners' sugar

White Chocolate Raspberry Cupcakes

■ Place 16 mini silicone muffin cups on a baking sheet.

■ Put the butter, superfine sugar, flour, baking powder, and egg in a bowl and beat with a handheld electric mixer until light and creamy. Stir in the chopped chocolate and divide among the cups.

■ Bake in a preheated oven, at 350°F, for 10–12 minutes, or until risen and just firm. Let stand in the cups for 2 minutes, then transfer to a wire rack to cool completely.

■ Make the topping by putting the raspberries in a bowl and crushing with a fork. Put the cream cheese and confectioners' sugar into a separate bowl and beat until smooth. Stir the crushed raspberries into the mixture until lightly combined but not completely blended. Spoon over the tops of the cakes and decorate with the chocolate curls.

FOR THOSE WITH A SWEET TOOTH

For marshmallow cream cakes, make the cakes opposite and let cool. Using a teaspoon, take a deep scoop out of the center of the cakes and spread a little raspberry preserves, jelly, or jam into the bottoms. Lightly toast 16 marshmallows and push one into the center of each cake. Whip 1 cup heavy cream with 1 tablespoon sifted confectioners' sugar and put in a pastry bag fitted with a ½ inch star tip. Pipe swirls up, around and over the marshmallows. Sprinkle with pink sugar sprinkles to decorate.

MAKES 24 SQUARES

Preparation time 25 minutes, plus cooling
Cooking time 55 minutes

INGREDIENTS

1 1¾ sticks salted butter, softened, plus extra for greasing

2 1¾ cups pitted dates, chopped

3 ⅔ cup heavy cream

4 2 teaspoons vanilla extract

5 3 eggs

PANTRY

⅔ cup water; ¾ cup firmly packed light brown sugar; ½ cup superfine sugar; 1⅓ cups all-purpose flour; 1¾ teaspoons baking powder

Caramel & Date Squares

◾ Grease and line an 11 × 7 inch shallow baking pan with nonstick parchment paper. Put 1 cup of the dates in a saucepan with the water and bring to a boil. Reduce the heat and cook gently for 5 minutes or until the dates are pulpy. Turn into a bowl and let cool. Put the cream, brown sugar, and 6 tablespoons of the butter into a small saucepan and heat gently until the sugar dissolves. Bring to a boil and boil for 5 minutes or until thickened and caramelized. Let cool.

◾ Put the remaining butter into a bowl with the superfine sugar, vanilla extract, and eggs, sift in the flour and baking powder, and beat with a handheld electric mixer until pale and creamy. Beat in the cooked dates and ½ cup of the caramel mixture. Turn into the pan and level the surface. Sprinkle with the remaining dates.

◾ Bake in a preheated oven, at 350°F, for 25 minutes, or until just firm. Spoon the remaining caramel on top and return to the oven for 15 minutes, until the caramel has firmed. Transfer to a wire rack to cool.

TRY IT WITH GLAZED APPLES

For glazed apple slices, grease the pan as opposite. Put 1½ sticks salted softened butter, ¾ cup plus 2 tablespoons superfine sugar, 1⅔ cups all-purpose flour, sifted, 2 teaspoons baking powder, 1 teaspoon ground allspice, and 3 eggs in a bowl and beat with a handheld electric mixer until smooth and creamy. Stir in ½ cup golden raisins and spread in the pan. Core and slice 2 small red apples and sprinkle them over the surface. Bake as opposite for 40 minutes or until just firm. Put ½ cup apple juice into a saucepan and heat until reduced to about 1 tablespoon. Cool and mix with ⅔ cup confectioners' sugar, sifted, until smooth. Drizzle the glaze over the cake.

MAKES 16

Preparation time 20 minutes, plus cooling
Cooking time 12 minutes

INGREDIENTS

1	5 tablespoons salted butter, softened

2	1 egg

3	3 tablespoons limoncello liqueur

4	5 tablespoons lemon curd

5	6 tablespoons unsalted butter, softened

PANTRY

⅓ cup superfine sugar; ½ cup all-purpose flour;
½ teaspoon baking powder; finely grated zest
of 1 lemon, plus 1 tablespoon of the juice; ⅓ cup
confectioners' sugar, plus extra for dusting

Lemon & Limoncello Cupcakes

■ Place 16 mini silicone muffin cups on a baking sheet.

■ Put the salted butter, superfine sugar, flour, lemon zest, and egg into a bowl and beat with a handheld electric mixer until light and creamy. Divide among the cups.

■ Bake in a preheated oven, at 350°F, for 10–12 minutes until risen and just firm. Leat stand in the cups for 2 minutes, then transfer to a wire rack to cool. Drizzle 2 tablespoons of the limoncello over the cakes and let cool completely.

■ Reserve 2 tablespoons of the lemon curd and spread the remainder over the cakes with a spatula.

■ Make the icing by putting the unsalted butter, confectioners' sugar, reserved limoncello, reserved lemon curd, and the lemon juice in a bowl and beating well until smooth and creamy. Put into a pastry bag fitted with a star tip and pipe swirls on top of each cake. Serve lightly dusted with confectioners' sugar.

TRY A DIFFERENT FRUIT

For rhubarb & orange cupcakes, make the cake as opposite, using the finely grated zest of ½ orange instead of lemon. Divide among the cups. Cut 2 rhubarb stalks into thin diagonal slices and toss with 4 teaspoons superfine sugar and a good pinch of ground ginger. Pile on top of the cakes and sprinkle with 2 tablespoons crushed slivered almonds. Bake as opposite and serve dusted with confectioners' sugar.

Preparation time 10 minutes
Cooking time 25 minutes

INGREDIENTS

1	1¼ sticks salted butter, softened
2	3 eggs
3	1 teaspoon almond extract
4	½ cup chopped mixed nuts
5	⅓ cup mixed dried fruit

PANTRY

⅔ cup firmly packed light brown sugar; 1⅔ cups all-purpose flour; 1½ cups baking powder

Fruit & Nut Cupcakes

■ Line two 12-cup muffin pans with 18 paper cupcake liners. Put the butter, sugar, flour, baking powder, eggs, and almond extract into a bowl and beat with a handheld electric mixer for 1–2 minutes, until light and creamy.

■ Add the chopped nuts and dried fruit and stir until evenly combined. Divide the cake batter among the paper liners.

■ Bake in a preheated oven, at 350°F, for 25 minutes, until risen and just firm to the touch. Transfer to a wire rack to cool.

INDEX

PICTURE CREDITS

Photography copyright © Octopus Publishing Group / Stephen Conroy 7, 9, 27, 49, 57, 61, 65, 67, 69, 107, 109, 113, 135, 145, 159, 161, 167; Will Heap 5, 20–21, 29, 31, 35, 41, 51, 59, 83, 85, 97, 123, 127, 139, 143, 147, 153, 156–157, 165, 173, 175, 177, 179, 181, 183, 185, 187; Neil Mersh 39, 55, 111; David Munns 71, 81, 91, 119, 163, 171; Emma Neish 62–63, 75; Lis Parsons 43, 77, 103; Gareth Sambidge 189; William Shaw 6, 8, 33, 37, 45, 53, 73, 79, 88–89, 95, 101, 105, 115, 117, 120–121, 125, 129, 131, 133, 137, 149, 151, 155, 169; Simon Smith 93; Ian Wallace 23, 25, 47, 87, 99, 141.